BRAND WINS!

REPUTATION MANAGEMENT IN A DIGITAL AGE
SECOND EDITION

STEVE CARR

CONTENTS

INTRODUCTION: MULTI-GENERATIONAL MARKETING

Reputation matters.

A long career in corporate consulting, including crisis management, rebranding, initial public offerings, and new product launches, has proven this to me every day. The winners in the business world treat their shareholders, employees, and customers right, and receive benefits accordingly. It's true on a personal level too. The experiences of my two Millennial children brought this home very recently.

My son is a philosophy major who didn't want to work in an office, so he joined the Brotherhood of Electrical Workers' apprenticeship program to become a union electrician. As with most union systems, work opportunities for the journeymen are typically based on first-come, first-served basis among individuals who post their availability with the union. But—not exactly. Senior people always stress to apprentices the importance of their reputation in the hiring process, as individuals with poor work habits or sloppy skills also can become among the first to be laid off. Contractors quickly come to gauge the quality of the individual offering his or her services, and union instructors and leaders advise newbies to be conscious of their vocational reputation from day one. This is a group that takes the "Brotherhood" in the name very seriously. My son quickly established his reputation as a smart, hard-working apprentice and was performing quality control for a major contractor—a job often reserved for a journeyman.

My daughter is a corporate trainer working for a large, non-U.S.-based consulting firm with Fortune 500 clients. She's an introvert who became an extrovert to work with clients—much like Dad! And guess who at her office is getting the tough assignments and overseas travel, coveted projects in New Delhi and Bangkok. Her skills and work ethic quickly made her the "go-to" person when something has to be done well and efficiently.

Your reputation is your brand, whether individually or as a corporation. And while intangible, is probably worth more than any brick and mortar you may own.

Whether you are a Baby Boomer or Gen Z, if you are a business owner, entrepreneur, corporate executive, or investor—or intend to be one of these—this book is for you.

I wrote it for one simple reason. As an adviser to companies large and small, local and international, private and public, I have seen countless dollars wasted on branding campaigns that accomplished nothing.

Here's why: When the value of an enterprise has been diminished (for any number of reasons), capital raisings become toxic financings and searches for merger partners fail dismally. While this can lead to some lucrative crisis work—as it has for me through the years—it's frustrating to deal with existential threats that could have been avoided with better decision-making. I finally felt compelled to write my ideas down in book-length form. Speeches, panel appearances, and white papers on this topic were no longer enough. Therefore, this book speaks to not only what you *should* do to grow, but what you should *not* do.

Classic example: In mid-2023, the Ivy League-educated marketing execs at Anheuser-Busch® sought a younger market for Bud Light®, a working person's brand and the best-selling beer in America, by celebrating a year of "girlhood" with a transgender influencer who posted an Instagram video of her picture: a personalized can while reclining in a bathtub. The immediate negative reaction from loyal celebrity fans and dedicated Bud Light drinkers tanked Anheuser-Busch stock, a $5 billion decline. The marketing execs had to be cashiered in short order due to a vote of no-confidence from senior management. A series of wobbly statements and patriotic videos failed to pacify the beer drinkers shocked at the sudden turn in tone, spokespersons, and values once evinced by the brand.

The moves intended to add value to the historic brand name instead turned out to be tone deaf and remarkably value destructive. Bud Light sales were down by double digits, with Coors Light® and Miller Lite® benefiting by corresponding amounts. Clearly, the social media misstep demonstrated a failure by marketing management to understand and appreciate the brand's core audience, and a botched attempt to expand that core base to younger, different customers.

In contrast, a successful brand update nodding to the #MeToo movement, which easily could have been a disaster, occurred when the Formula One® auto-racing circuit eliminated the "grid girls," the scantily clad, attractive young women hired to work on the sidelines and podiums of the male-dominated sporting events worldwide. "This custom does not resonate with our brand values and clearly is at odds with modern-day societal norms," the organization said in its announcement. While many fans were disappointed, the girls themselves, who were apparently well-paid and well-treated, took their newfound joblessness in stride and were good sports about the news. Formula One went on to be the star of a popular Netflix® series and to launch major new races in Miami, Austin, and Las Vegas.

At the end of the day, any business, no matter how large or small, needs to be on top of its reputation risks, and needs to have a crisis plan in its back pocket. In both the above examples, the organizations involved chose to engage with social issues, voluntarily. One had a poor grasp on risks and rewards of dealing with issues such as transgender rights, and on its relationships with its core markets. The other organization had a keen knowledge of both.

Throughout these pages, you'll find reminders to focus on your brand values. The second major theme is to focus on the endgame of your business venture—whether you are still writing a business plan, seeking financing, running a fast-growing venture, managing a mature business, or thinking about retirement and needing an exit.

Every day, a huge amount of commentary is poured forth on how to fund or organize a startup company. Many of these teachings are quite valuable.

In contrast, relatively little copy is devoted to the idea that, sooner or later, this startup or mature company must be sold to someone. Too many families have no heirs prepared to assume control of the business. Too few management teams have strong successors ready to get the company to the next level. My point of view is very simple, but its wisdom has been proven time and time again through observation of successful and less-than-successful business outcomes: *Have your value-creation plan and your exit strategies in front of you when you begin your enterprise.*

Sooner or later, your focus on wealth creation will turn to a focus on wealth preservation. This means a value-creation plan needs to be in place long before you think about closing on the sale of the business.

Please consider this volume to be your handbook on how to achieve these goals. Because the essence of creating and maintaining value is a healthy brand reputation!

Ask yourself: What if I could develop my brand sufficiently to realize my personal, professional, or corporate dreams? With the right mindset, approaches, and tools, you *can* do this. Others have. The stories in this book are true. In some cases, individuals asked for anonymity, but the circumstances of these individuals or work situations described herein are real. And they achieved their dreams by building a powerful personal or corporate brand.

This is the case whether they were working in tech startups, mature companies, nonprofits and NGOs, big banks, or consulting firms. The people who have succeeded, interviewed at length in these pages, have valuable experience to impart. They're quoted here so you can avoid their mistakes and gain the benefit of their hard-won wisdom.

Many of these businesspeople were in situations in which they needed to grow the revenues and profitability of their brands over time, work through obstacles such as the need for capital, and suffered setbacks such as the unexpected loss of a major client along the way.

The steps as outlined here sound straightforward. Of course, if it were easy, everyone would be doing it. To implement a strategy, you often must break out of tried-and-true patterns of thinking. As the leaders quoted herein all note, breaking out of the pack is the enabler of creating a sterling reputation and a noteworthy brand. And that intangible known as the brand is essential to your value creation plan and your profitable exit.

By this point you are probably thinking to yourself that any entrepreneur is focused on a market opportunity, on hiring, on the building blocks of maintenance and growth. And you would be right. These are your areas of concern, and I leave them to you. My remit is to help you originate and develop a brand that enhances your personal, professional, and corporate reputation, thereby creating value beyond what you could normally achieve. My professional life has been spent helping people build enterprise value through intangibles such as corporate reputation and investor relations. This expertise goes beyond the more easily measured criteria, such as Earnings Before Interest, Taxes, and Depreciation (the all-important EBITDA) also discussed in this book.

Why? Because a nexus of intangibles such as an engaged employee workforce, good reputation, compliance, and transparency often contribute more to a company's valuation than the more tangible bricks and mortar, particularly in the aftermath of COVID-19 and the global decline in office occupancy rates. Appreciating how the intangibles help add value to a business is an advantage many of your peers and competitors will not enjoy.

The collective examples in this book speak to one profound truth: Set out to build a strong brand with a good reputation, and you will be required change your behavior to realize your dreams. Count on it. The stories that follow highlight three key themes:

- *Successful people get intentional.* When I first started planning to leave a full-time position and abandon the safety of a paycheck, I became paralyzed by analysis. Decision dates, how to set up an LLC, when to leave, when to print business cards, when to inform trusted prospects and partners, how to build my own referral network of business rather than relying on trade associations and conferences for leads.... It put a brake on my process for months. Looking back, it's clear that I really wasn't intentional about getting started. Lesson learned. You must be motivated by strong aspirations to change your behavior. Only later did that happen for me. Intentions and aspirations are not the principal focus of this volume, but if you need more information on the subject, a good source is Dr. Wayne Dyer's transformational book, *The Power of Intention*.

- *Have a sense of urgency.* This point is closely related to the above. When I finally became intentional about achieving my aspirations, I performed most of my critical tasks in one weekend: arranging a financial safety net, choosing a logo from online graphic design sources, considering social media marketing strategies such as setting up my own YouTube channel and podcast, and reaching out with trusted sources to discuss my plans and timeline.

- *Incremental progress is OK.* This theme may seem counterintuitive to the above two points but is a realistic experience. Not every account win will be big; many accounts will be hourly or project rather than ongoing retainer. There will be bad debts and slow pays. In sum, your aspirations won't happen in a day, and much of your progress will be over time or incremental. Look at your progress in milestones, and that will help you get a realistic sense of your progress or lack thereof.

The point is, aspirations need to be actionable to be meaningful, and they all begin with the germ of an idea. Often this germ is perceiving a need in a marketplace, or the need to replace lost income, or some other dissatisfaction with the existing order of things. Time and time again, we will see examples in this book of individuals and organizations who aspire to new goals only when the pain of staying the same becomes greater than the perceived risk of making a change.

Aspirations are characterized by the following: (1) a role model one wants to emulate; (2) a goal that motivates one to act; and (3) changes in behavior to achieve the new goals. So often, a change in behavior is critical, whether you are an unemployed accountant, a graduate student looking for your first full-time job, the founder of a web-design business, or an employee at a Fortune 500 company. Taken in this context, the main purpose of this book is to foster change.

Because the reader here may come from many different professional situations, this book is organized in quick-to-read sections that are easy to capture. If you're not considering an IPO, skip chapter seven. If you are dealing with how to sell a family-owned business, or how to face a franchise-threatening crisis, jump to chapters five and nine, respectively, to access the information you need. No harm, no foul.

Chapters one through four analyze the value of intangibles such as a solid brand and good reputation, while later chapters discuss specific areas of concern such as crisis management or improving your company's reputation when your industry, such as cannabis, may struggle with regulatory and public image issues. The final chapter is a summary of lessons that could benefit leaders of any size company or any industry.

And so, appreciate the teachings in the next ten chapters. Feel free to share your own experiences with me via email at sdcarr146@gmail.com.

1

MANAGING IN A FULL-DISCLOSURE WORLD

Whether you are a growing company seeking to go public, a young company seeking capital, or a mature company pondering expansion, each business eventually will be sold, closed, merged, go public, or go bankrupt.

Growing the valuation of public and private companies, including the portfolio companies of private-equity firms, is a significant challenge, whether the markets are strong or whether the economy is moving at what economist Larry Kudlow calls "stall speed." This maximized value is summarized by what the professional investing class seeks, above-market returns named "alpha."

De-mystifying how to build the maximum sustainable valuation for your company is the key lesson of the next two chapters. I emphasize *sustainable* valuation. We've all seen highs in our 401(k) accounts or in particular investments in our favorite stocks, or even in the stock of the company that employs us. But is it *sustainable* over time? Sustained value is what counts in the end. Otherwise, when you are readying your endgame, there's really nothing left to sell.

The strategy for enhancing the valuation of undervalued companies is to put into place an active investor relations program. In short, financial communications have to be part of your reputation management considerations. Studies of buy-and-sell-side analysts and stock performance consistently reveal that good investor relations can add as much as 10% to the valuation of a company, or even more, while poor IR could detract as much as 17.5% from their valuation.

Telling the corporate story to the right type of investor is key to achieving the highest sustainable valuation. This is true of the Fortune 500 and the corner gas station. Yesterday's model of investor relations is similar to a shotgun approach or a large-scale ambush because it emphasizes reaching the largest audience. It fails to look at the financial trends typically employed by the buy-side investment community, specifically the bigger pension funds and institutional investors who call the shots for the sell-siders (the analysts we see quoted on CNBC and in the *Wall Street Journal* every day).

At the heart of the idea of growing value is transparency into the strategy, tactics, and financial performance of the company. Transparency is more than the latest corporate buzzword, although it is that too. It's the commitment to be transparent about corporate values, strengths, position in the marketplace, and even flaws. And it involves the duty to provide timely, truthful updates, at least an ethical duty if not a legal one.

Update whom? Potentially, any stakeholder in the company, from investors to communities, industry analysts, employees, regulators, legislators, and of course customers and prospects.

This range of stakeholders, which goes far beyond the actual shareholders of the corporation, is a list that motivated several presidential candidates in 2020 to actually propose legislation requiring corporations to be operated for the benefit of such audiences. For reasons that would fill a legal tome or countless law journals, requiring this additional set of obligations as an onerous piece of regulation is a bad idea. Allowing organizations or individuals to have a controlling voice in corporate operations when the needs of those parties may be antithetical to the actual owners and managers of the corporation is a recipe for corporate and economic disaster. However, listening to activists is almost always a good idea. That doesn't mean boards of directors or CEOs should always act on these dissenting ideas, as many of them are remarkably unrealistic or even harmful.

Transparency is closely linked to the legal concept of materiality. When courts look at whether there has been insider trading in a company's stock, or if an executive has improperly withheld information that should have been shared with the investing public, they look at whether the information was material. Is it information that an investor would like to know before investing or continuing to invest?

Some examples of what public companies are required to disclose but sometimes don't—or disclose in a misleading fashion, or disclose very slowly—include but are not limited to:

- Quarterly and annual earnings
- Declaration of dividends, stock splits, share repurchases
- Changes in senior management
- Mergers, acquisitions, tender offers
- Major new products likely to affect the top line and bottom line

- Major borrowings or sales of additional securities
- Secondary offerings of stock
- Addition of major new customers and contracts, or loss of same

Privately held companies are legally required to announce none of the above, but it may well be worth their while to do so in the interest of meeting the information needs of their stakeholders. New sources of revenue, or loss of these, is especially important to the investor or the prospective buyer of a company for sale.

Transparency as a value is permeating corporate America, and not only in its dialogue with the outside. For example, employees have been working from home for several decades now, a cultural shift only made possible by the technology of laptops, smartphones, and VPNs (Virtual Private Networks). The policy was made because it is family-friendly and pet-friendly, and certainly aids in recruiting. It cuts the cost of office space as well, sometimes dramatically.

During the COVID-19 pandemic, office work became remote work and millions became comfortable working in their sweatpants from home. City centers were hollowed out as offices emptied, and the office worker support systems that fast-food and fine dining locales, shops, transit systems, and business services relied on were suddenly lost. But the tide is now beginning to shift back. There are multiple reasons for this, but the big reason is transparency.

Increasingly, margin-pressed corporations want to know where their employees are, and how they are performing, which is much harder to do when people are working remotely. Corporate cultures also are much easier to create and maintain in person than online. The return to the office is most pronounced now at the larger companies, but it is a trend that is trickling down to the smaller companies as well. Understandably, in-office work is unpopular with many workers who had developed more convenient methods of pet care, elder care, and child care. Also, the cities desperate for property tax revenue from full office buildings, mass transit lines that need paying riders, and small businesses that depend upon office workers are anxious to see people back in urban centers. Clearly, much of the business from the city center has shifted to the urban neighborhoods or suburbs where people are working from home and spending more time and money at the local gyms, coffee shops and restaurants, so the transition is not necessary a total loss for some states.

The back-and-forth between home and office, with ensuring dislocations, will continue for years, probably in a stalemate similar to conditions today. Behind the scenes, mergers and acquisitions, as well as corporate compliance officers, will help drive the return-to-office push, in part because businesspeople relying on other business people requires full disclosure. Looking to sell your company? Steve Eschbach, president of the Naperville, Illinois, unit of Transworld Business Advisors, a national franchise specializing in buying and selling smaller companies, told me that one of the first questions buyers ask of sellers is: Who are your primary customers, vendors, and other third-party affiliations? The reason, explains Eschbach, is these business relationships are paramount to determining risk and therefore, the value of the company.

Ultimately, these relationships are part of the brand. They determine not only the value of the enterprise but whether or not the company will be sold. This is true of Eschbach's small business clientele and of the global giants. Goldman Sachs, the gold standard of international investment banking, maintains a reputational risk committee whose remit includes business and client decisions that could cause damage to the firm's reputation. (Think Russian oligarchs under sanctions, convicted felons such as Jeffrey Epstein, and industries with dodgy connections.) Transparency is a mandate that includes the seller, the buyer, and their business advisors.

Accountability and transparency are twin concepts. They cannot be divorced. Companies want more accountability, and increased transparency contributes to improved accountability. One must have clarity about what is happening in order to hold others accountable for their performance. Senior corporate executives must be held accountable by boards and investors for company performance and stock price, and the lower echelons must be held accountable for their areas of responsibility as well. But first, the performance must be transparent.

The cynical view of this is expressed in the definition of IPO, Initial Public Offering, in Jason Zweig's *The Devil's Financial Dictionary*. "Initial Public Offering, or the first sale of a company's stock by private owners who know everything about it to public buyers who know nothing about it. Marketed to the outside investors as an opportunity to get in on the ground floor of a growing business, the typical IPO instead presents the greatest opportunity to the insiders who are selling, because the associated hype enables them to cash out at inflated prices. IPO can thus be more accurately be said to stand for 'insider's private opportunity,' 'imaginary profits only,' or 'it's probably overpriced.'"

In the government sector, Sunshine Laws enacted decades ago predate the corporate trend and mandate government decisions be made in a manner that is open to the public. Yet secret decision-making continues to be done, and it always draws media attention.

In mid-2019, when actor Jussie Smollett manufactured an attack on himself as a publicity stunt, the Chicago prosecutor's office allowed him to get off with no prison sentence, despite the considerable police resources that had been dedicated to his case. The continuing controversy over what Smollett did, and the local government reaction that smacked of favoritism, resulted in his court records being unsealed, though they were released to the public in a redacted form. The continuing controversy eventually forced a local judge to appoint an independent official to investigate the possible cover-up as well as the underlying facts.

Bottom line: numerous third-party groups will continue to monitor and advocate for government transparency at all levels, a sure sign the battle is far from won. In coming decades, this trend will generate contentious public issues affecting individuals and companies of all sizes.

On a national scale, the decisions by President Lyndon Johnson, government officials, and senior military officials that led to the war in Vietnam were cloaked in secrecy and misrepresentation. As documented in his landmark book, ironically titled *The Best and The Brightest*, David Halberstam clearly identified the misrepresentations involved. "There was one other important thing the President and his aides decided on April 1: although they were changing the nature of the American commitment and the mission of the Marines, there was to be no announcement of it ... James Reston of the *Times* was later to write that Lyndon Johnson escalated the war by stealth; he could not have been more right."

The disconnect between the optimistic information generated by the government about the prosecution of the war and the grim reality Americans saw on television famously became known as the Credibility Gap. One could make a good argument that this horrific situation began the decades-long slide of trust in American institutions that persists today. And it has continued into the 2020s as the Fed committed a series of mistakes on inflation and interest rates after the pandemic shutdowns, and the Biden administration painted a rosy picture of the economy.

Transparency is a powerful concept for individuals and businesses alike. After accused sex offender and billionaire financier Jeffrey Epstein was found dead in prison, U.S. District Judge Richard M. Berman allowed 16 women who say he abused them their day in court. Why the unusual opportunity? The most-quoted phrase in the media as the judge defended his decision to hold a public hearing was that the extraordinary event would "promote transparency."

Transparency is most often discussed in terms of publicly held companies such as Boeing®. In truth, this is insufficient. Privately held or even family-owned companies that want to be taken seriously and have a backdrop of credibility, should emulate their publicly-held brethren. Some who have adopted this philosophy even publish financial or quarterly reports that can be shared with customers, employees, and other interested parties. Granted, these documents are considerably abridged from the 10Ks and 10Qs of the public world, but they contain some financial trend information and color on the trends in the business and the industry. This positions the company as a serious player within its category and certainly would help position it to raise capital, to be sold, or to go public.

Moreover, buyers want to know not only your client lists and historical financials, but plans to compete now and later. If you are a dry cleaner, for example, why do customers frequent your place of business rather than the other dry cleaners in the area? With the advent of Tide® dry cleaning operations, which offer 24-hour service and Sunday hours, a major question for the small independents is how they will compete against this large national brand based on a consumer household product.

This is just another example demonstrating that to succeed in your aspirations, you will need to be very realistic and very, VERY intentional.

Aspiration to succeed is a uniquely American value that has inspired the tech entrepreneurs of Silicon Valley, as well as the financial geniuses of Wall Street and Middle American entrepreneurs. The motive has inspired companies around the world to replicate the American escalator of success. Yet too often our literature and personal or professional planning ignores the end point of virtually all companies, which is that at some point in their history they will be sold. In fact, many companies are sold more than once. The beginning point of any planning, whether we are leading public companies selling shares to the investing public, or starting a restaurant, growing a chain of fitness clubs, or joining a startup, should be: How do we want to exit? And understanding this timeline and goal may well change in the course of your working life; in fact, it may change many times. The key to sustaining a career and a business is to manage with this reality in mind as you ponder ways of accessing talent, capital, and customers, and maximizing the value of your brand.

This all builds to the endgame further on up the road. How do you want to exit the business? If your plan is to sell to another business, or a private equity firm, or to your employees, great—but who are these likely buyers, specifically? Why would they be interested? Do they have the resources to pay you? Should you retain a licensed investment bank or one of many unlicensed business brokers to find a suitable buyer for a success fee?

Perhaps, instead, your business is in a fashionable category and you may seek to go public, offering shares to the world at large. Or finally, perhaps there are no plans to exit in your lifetime, and the issue of succession will be left up to family or board members.

"I had an exit plan in mind from the get-go," said the owner of one successful franchise. "When I started, I was one of two franchises in my area, but now I'm one of five." He prospered by collaborating with the new owners in their respective geographic areas and creating an informal business team to share leads and work on deals. Now he is in a favorable position to transition management of the business to another like-minded entrepreneur.

Of course, companies and organizations also have goals, and such goals contribute to their overall brand strategy. A corporate goal could be adding ten cents to share price on a sustainable basis, improving the quality of a product as measured by customer feedback, or finding a buyer for the company who will infuse cash and protect the jobs of current employees. Many corporate brands or cultures are in fact held up as aspirational to many others, in the same way that sports figures (Michael Jordan), business celebrities (Richard Branson), humanitarians (Jimmy Carter), and other role models in public life become, willingly or not, people to emulate.

It must be made clear that we are not talking about skills improvement, but goals and aspirations. Skills improvement does not change behavior. Time and time again, corporate behemoths as well as many fledgling companies have invested time and training dollars in skills improvement only to see no effect in changing the corporate culture. Of course, adding new skills and improving existing skills is important to individuals and employers alike. These may include soft skills designed to improve supervisory abilities or the so-called hard skills involving software, hardware, or other technical expertise. But the direct result in behavior is generally negligible. As management icon Peter Drucker has said, "If you want something new, you have to stop doing something old."

2

DE-MYSTIFYING SHAREHOLDER VALUE

The practice of communicating with the investment community—the professional discipline referred to as investor relations or IR—is a mix of regulatory and voluntary activities, interacting with current investors, prospective investors, analysts, and business and trade journalists. The role is ubiquitous in the public company and private equity world. Within the practice, the members of its trade group, the National Investor Relations Institute (NIRI), refer to themselves as IROs, or Investor Relations Officers; in the shorthand of Wall Street, most analysts simply call them "the IRs." NIRI defines investor relations as "a strategic management responsibility which integrates finance, communications, marketing and securities law compliance," to give you a feel for the challenge.

At the heart of a good IR practice is transparency, using the state-of-the-art digital and social media techniques now available to practitioners, as well as traditional communication channels. For the financier considering upping the game on investor relations, it is strategy rather than these tactics that must be considered first. There is a host of strategic issues that must be engaged to enhance value from an investor relations standpoint.

THE NEW MODEL FOR POSITIONING AND MESSAGING

Positioning and messaging—major parts of the thinking companies employ as they rebrand, launch new products, or enter new categories—are the keys to raising their profile and exposure in the capital markets. The positioning and message will vary by company and industry, as will the strength of the company's brand reputation, all with the goal of accurately and effectively presenting a company to the investment community. A dedicated campaign with consistent, easily understandable messaging typically results in a substantial increase in investor awareness and active institutional involvement.

Money managers agree the four greatest drivers of shareholder value are revenue growth, competitive advantage, margin improvement, and a cohesive strategic plan. One of the most important aspects of building shareholder value is the management team's dedication to creating, maintaining, and communicating these drivers through targeted, relevant, and consistent messages that demonstrate how and why value is being created. In recessionary times there is a rotation to defensive stocks, but over time investors gravitate again to earnings growth. Often there is an emphasis on fast growth, not necessarily profitability.

A major part of the analysis is to identify and analyze corporate peers and competitors to determine a company's relative investment merit against comparable companies in the market. The next step is to create the investable messages that will be incorporated in all communications with the Street. Having an appreciation of the financial drivers of value is not enough to achieve consistently superior returns. Sustained performance requires a commitment to communicating management's goals and the strategic steps for reaching those goals. The success of a company's management team will be measured by its ability to earn cash returns above the company's cost of capital. After all, the capital markets expect corporations to not only generate positive earnings and sales growth, but also to provide an appropriate return on investment.

I've looked at thousands of investor presentations and almost always offer the same observation to the creator: they are lacking at least one critical page. There needs to be one page, either upfront or at the end of the presentation as a summary, that highlights why someone should put money into this company. A market niche. A must-have management team. Solid IP (intellectual property). A high growth curve in its end-markets that the company is well-positioned to ride. Whatever the reasons, they need to appear in plain, easy-to-grasp language.

I think the reason this page is so often missing is precisely that these reasons are often so difficult for a founder or owner to put into words. This is where outside professionals—IR people, accountants, lawyers—often can be invaluable, with their distance as third-party experts. Nobody knows the business as well as the founder or owner, true. That is a powerful source of vision and messaging. Yet these originators will often need an advisor who can serve as translator, and ultimately, megaphone. The belief that a good idea or a good product will sell itself is one I have encountered for decades. I have never seen It proven in practice. Never. Yet the belief continues to exist, especially among engineering and software creators, and it has been the death knell of many otherwise worthwhile endeavors.

What needs to be in a presentation? Most venture capital firms have their own preferences which are usually shared publicly as an outline so people seeking funds know what to expect; Sequoia Capital has a particularly good one. In my experience the "must-haves" are:

- Headline (a "grabber" to attract immediate attention)
- Description of business (what the company does)
- Product or service demo(s), if applicable
- Size of market
- Ability to scale, if applicable
- Management team bios
- Amount of capital sought and uses of funds
- How investors will make money
- Exit plans (IPO, or sale—perhaps to partners, employees, competitors, or private equity)
- Timelines for the above
- Closing statement (typically thank you and Q&A period)

Above and beyond these, presenters can include anecdotes and stories that highlight key points, which often add interest to the pitch. One software company I worked with had a founder who simply abhorred paper and from a young age had made it one of his life's missions to go paperless. While not exactly world peace, the goal always attracted the attention of investors in the room.

INVESTOR TARGETING

Taking the corporate story to the right type of investor is key to achieving the highest sustainable valuation. The old model of investor relations is similar to a shotgun approach or a large-scale ambush, because it focuses on reaching the largest audience and fails to look at the financial methods employed by the majority of the buy-side investment community. The new and more effective model is to integrate financial analysis, valuation metrics, and investor communications. Covering all avenues of quantitative and qualitative targeting methods, a solid institutional target program will uncover fund managers and independent money managers who seek companies with the same financial characteristics as the company in question. The key to success is to focus on identifying the most logical investors, communicating the value drivers that are most relevant, and then introducing management to these targeted investors. The outcome is to bring the company's story vividly to the attention of the fund managers, analysts, and investors most likely to act.

PERCEPTION STUDIES

Knowing the issues that are important to the Street is the first step in a successful investor relations program. Often prior to an IPO, and post-IPO, a perception study is a useful tool. This is a sample of leading investment professionals to capture the current mindset of existing shareholders and peer group owners regarding the company's reputation and strategy. Using perception studies, misconceptions in the marketplace can be identified to determine what is fueling the perception gap between management and the Street.

Depending upon the scope of the research and the number

of influential analysts in the industry, the study can be accomplished in a matter of weeks. Phone or in-person surveys are best; email and Web methods tend to be too limiting. Using agreed-upon questions, the interviewer—an IR practitioner or paid researcher—determines parties to be interviewed, conducts the interview, and transcribes the verbatim comments of the interviewee along with written summaries and conclusions.

Perception studies are a primary source of first-hand feedback from analysts and portfolio managers regarding their investment in your company. Often, senior management is unaware of true investor sentiment, whether positive or negative, since this candid information is often times not readily available. The goal of the survey is to gather impressions, feedback, and assumptions from a collection of investors, and assess them, providing actionable conclusions. Actionable research is the hallmark of a well-conducted perception study. These conclusions will arm corporate advisers and management with a framework for all future communications.

PUBLIC RELATIONS

Sometimes one of the strongest foundations for a solid IR program is a good PR program. This is especially true for private-equity firms seeking to build the value of a portfolio company in advance of a planned sale, leveraged buy-out (LBO), or public offering. It is certainly true for a company hoping to go public. Leaders in academia and communications research often testify to the fact that the credibility of the news is eight times greater than that of paid advertising. Given the furor over "fake news," the credibility aspect of this assertion is certainly no longer true, but the value of so-called "earned media" (media coverage that is not sponsored by advertising) is undeniable.

Customers and stakeholders may be impressed by dazzling full-page ads, clever commercials, and even customized direct mail pieces. Yet, the fact the company "pays for play" in each of these instances is a barrier to complete credibility. Public relations can increase visibility with current and prospective shareholders and improves senior management's corporate reputation. Editorial coverage is one of the most effective ways to build brand awareness, reach prospective investors and customers, establish credibility, and influence the decision-making-process to shorten the product sales cycle.

There is no substitute for third-party endorsements of a company's or an industry's brand, products, and services. In fact, at different times, the European Private Equity Roundtable, the British Capital Association, and the European Venture Capital Association have conducted searches for a public relations agency to represent the private equity industry. This is simply more proof the business community worldwide understands the value of brand and reputation, and that these factors often regarded as intangible do in fact contribute to value.

In short, the flow and management of communications with the investment community is an important and ongoing task. In today's crowded capital markets, a company must maintain an ongoing dialogue with investors that recognizes a company's business fundamentals. That is how to maximize valuation for undervalued, unknown, or untested companies.

3

REPUTATION MANAGEMENT IN A DIGITAL AGE

Warren Buffett, the founder of Berkshire Hathaway, the company that has made him both a billionaire and a business sage, is often quoted on the subject of corporate reputation. A man with a strong reputation for personal and professional integrity himself, he has often observed, "It takes 20 years to build a reputation and five minutes to ruin it. If you think about that, you'll do things differently." Of Berkshire Hathaway specifically, he has told people, "We can afford to lose money—even a lot of money. But we can't afford to lose reputation—even a shred of reputation."

Long before most, Buffett understood the link between corporate value and corporate reputation.

Corporate reputation management protects a company from economic harm by differentiating it from peers and by instituting sound behavioral practices, and then communicating them to its whole universe—employees, vendors, suppliers, bankers, consultants, shareholders, media, local communities, rating agencies, financial and industry analysts, regulators, legislators, advocacy groups, customers, prospects, and trade associations—basically, anyone who helps influence and determine the company's future.

And you must reach these influencers with one voice.

Corporate reputations are best managed holistically—an approach that recognizes companies have many public-facing facets, such as products and services, capital needs, customer interactions, and a social media presence. It also takes advantage of the synergies between constituencies who often have different information needs. Another plus to this philosophy is avoiding the conflicting messages that can occur when responsibility for each constituency resides in a different part of the country.

If you think maintenance of a good corporate reputation is hard, consider the damage done when it is broken and the difficulty of repairing trust with your key audiences after a breach.

After all, public trust in American institutions—from Congress, to the media, to business—has been dropping for decades, and reputation is all about trust.

Ask yourself, what is the perception of American business? When was the last time a movie featured a company as the hero instead of the villain? And perhaps it's no surprise, as so many trusted brands disappoint over time. Volkswagen misrepresented its emissions tests. British Petroleum polluted the Gulf of Mexico. Equifax hid a massive data breach exposing the personal information of 143 million consumers.

Every major player in the crypto world needed to recast its image after the FTX fraud allegations and bankruptcy crashed stock market valuations and confidence in the industry. "The problem they face is a massive drop-off of trust as holders of assets that have value," said Tom Wason, a consultant who works with industry leaders.

Now, what is the perception of your industry?

Your company?

You and your team?

If you don't know, now is the time to find out, perhaps by commissioning perception studies or holding focus groups with customers or blind (anonymous response) surveys with your employees. With today's technology, it's possible (if not always easy) to back responses with data. Get the facts. If you don't like what you hear, provide feedback and work on solutions.

Where corporate reputation is concerned, silence is not golden.

THE FIXERS

Political advisors and spokespeople have known this for years, especially since the Bill Clinton presidential years. The Clintons never left a charge unanswered, either responding directly themselves or indirectly through proxies.

In recent years, the term "fixer" has entered the mainstream vocabulary with the popularity of shows such as *Ray Donovan* and *Rabbit Hole* that deal with the intersection of politics, Hollywood, and finance.

A long-standing fictional character, Stone Barrington, in a series of novels by Stuart Woods, is employed by a prestigious law firm to handle cases with which it does not want to seem to be involved, typically for its well-heeled clients. Stone has become entangled with corporate take-overs, murder plots by the Russian mafia, and sensationalistic press coverage. In the novel *A Delicate Touch,* for example, he deals with election fraud, money laundering, organized crime, and at least three paramours.

Another similar character in the TV world is Ray Donovan, a Hollywood fixer who eventually relocates to New York City.

Heavily involved in addressing the problems of celebrities, media figures, and politicians, this long-running Showtime series is really more of a family and crime drama. Ray at times is portrayed somewhat as a thug, with a wooden baseball bat kept handy for personal defense. A strong portrayal by Liev Schreiber shows Ray overcome by personal demons, eventually consulting a therapist, which could become a life-saving consultation.

The public fascination with these corporate fixers continues unabated as Kiefer Sutherland plays a fixer with flexible ethics in *Rabbit Hole*. His machinations include defending a snack food manufacturer threatened with a new competing product by infiltrating allies who vomit during a taste test. He denies corporate espionage to an FBI financial crimes unit investigator. "Manipulating people, influencing markets, is what then?" demands the agent. "Consulting," Sutherland replies.

In the movie world, *Michael Clayton*, a film starring George Clooney, is predicated on a cover-up of a corporate crime. Like Stone Barrington, Michael handles problems his New York law firm and its clients do not want to be seen to be associated with. When a whistleblower threatens to blow up a major piece of litigation involving a huge pharmaceutical company, a threatened executive decides to bring in hired killers to remove not only the whistleblower but anyone else with knowledge of a corporate cover-up, including Michael. A strong cast and a classy production make the film compelling despite its somewhat far-fetched plot turns.

Are there real-life fixers? You bet. In fact, the world's financial center, London, has so many "professional enablers" it decided to regulate them with a special agency. Many of these lawyers, accountants, real-estate agents, and corporate service providers serve wealthy foreigners who need help navigating the byways of the city. In Russia they call them *polittekhnologs*.

Closer to home in the USA, the TV show *Scandal* was inspired by Judy Smith, who owns her own Washington, D.C.-based crisis management firm. Smith, a former deputy press secretary to George H.W. Bush, has done crisis communications for the likes of former D.C. mayor Marion Berry, the World Health Organization when it was responding to a SARS outbreak, and Monica Lewinsky after her affair with President Bill Clinton became public.

Like the fictional fixers, the real-world ones are often facing the media. Typically, they are New York-based. Jonathan Gasthalter became well-known for dealing with tough media situations defending Stephen Cohen and his hedge fund SAC Capital against insider trading charges. Michael Sitrick and his firm represented Harvey Weinstein during the time the Hollywood producer faced rape charges in Manhattan. Besieged celebrities and business figures alike turn to these spinmeisters when dark clouds gather.

Less savory characters such as President Trump's attorney Michael D. Cohen achieved a great deal of fame, with features such as the *Wall Street Journal* article in January 17, 2019 headlined, "Intelligence Dossier Puts Longtime Trump Fixer in Spotlight." Payments to former Trump mistresses and alleged bribery issues led to his indictment and a focus on the abilities of fixers to legally or illegally, and discreetly or not so discreetly, resolve potentially embarrassing issues for their principals.

Conversely, in the white-shoe banking world, H. Rodgin Cohen, known as Rodge, the senior chair at law firm Sullivan & Cromwell, was at the center of efforts to save Silicon Valley Bank and First Republic in 2023. His resume involves decades of working on banking crises, and during the Iran-contra affair of the Reagan years he served as an advisor to American banks that released Iranian funds as a condition to freeing the American hostages.

Note that a fixer is not necessarily a consigliere. This role was made famous in the *Godfather* movies, with Marlon Brando's chief advisor, Tom Hagen, played by Robert Duvall. In Italian, consigliere simply means "counselor," derived from "*consiglio*" or "advice." He is a right-hand man, like a fixer, but his value lies more in his capacity for thought than action and connections. Tom Hagen never wields the wooden bat himself.

In the real corporate world, maintaining a good corporate reputation tends to be less dramatic, and restoring one typically takes years of hard work with much back-and-forth. It's not as simple as holding a press conference and putting it behind you, although that can be a start.

As I alluded to earlier, reputation can be measured. Some large PR firms publish publicly available reports on public opinion of major institutions, corporations, and industry categories. The international PR firm, Edelman, generates a well-regarded survey rating trustworthiness of corporations. Private research firms, of which the best known is Oxford Metrica, do industry studies and reports commissioned by a company. You also can simply go to a research firm you know and trust to order up an online poll, focus group (a panel of people recruited for a small fee to offer opinions in a setting moderated by a professional researcher), or phone survey on an issue that is researchable.

Let's think about what you want to accomplish first. How does a good corporate reputation help your business? In many ways. Positive perceptions help:

- Attract new customers
- Attract investors

- Build brand awareness
- Build market share
- De-position competitors (excluding them from the competitor set for buyers)
- Enhance your credibility
- Retain existing customers
- Retain and attract employees
- Reduce the amount of money you need to spend on advertising
- Shorten the sales cycle

In short, it's no wonder the intangibles of a business can account for a substantial portion of its enterprise value. Think about how to create a backdrop of credibility for you and the company or brand you represent. Your communications options basically boil down to three main platforms. Let's take a quick overview of each.

First is traditional media. One immediately thinks of paid advertising in newspapers, TV, or radio. Yet this type of communication is very intrusive and can be expensive. Many clients, thinking radio ads are very inexpensive, have expressed shock when they actually saw what a radio budget in a major market such as Chicago can actually cost. Moreover, 68 million Americans have downloaded some type of ad-blocking software.

The death knell of paid advertising, though, is really the data analytics offered by social media. Paid traditional media advertising really does not document who saw what or read what. No wonder businesses of all sizes have migrated to the Web for its click-through ads, or text and video to reach mobile devices. Estimated audience reach and subscriber lists in traditional media are dwarfed in importance by real-time reports on the numbers and demographics of the audiences reached through social media. Stale information can't compete with constantly updated views of consumer behavior.

So-called "earned media" became a major public issue in 2016 when presidential candidate Donald Trump relied more on his one-on-one media interviews and huge rallies that, televised, multiplied their impact many times. Yet earned media is a term that has long been used to describe the results that appear online and in traditional media through the skills of public relations experts. Skilled at determining what is a good story and a good visual, these practitioners were long famous for their media connections and pitching savvy.

Social media has had a negative impact on the PR business as well as traditional advertising, and for the same reasons: lower costs, and more definitive reporting and tracking. Some PR firms have reported high growth in recent years and increased staffing, but if you look behind the curtains, the truth is more that they are staffing differently. Traditional PR experts focused on media relations are being replaced over time with writers versed in online copywriting and coders who create digital games, ads, and websites.

As dramatic as these changes have been in the world of marketing and communications, they may pale with the coming onset of AI. OpenAI's ChatGPT became a viral sensation upon introduction and quickly became the fastest growing app in the history of the internet, attracting one hundred million users with a year. The software has been used for menial chores such as tabulation and synopses, customer interactions that seem human, and medical diagnostics. People have used it to generate scripts, analyze vast amounts of customer data, do corporate training, and generate high-quality life-like simulations.

The debate about its uses can be dramatized by the Hollywood writers' strike this year, with writers arguing AI should be reserved for research and fact-checking, while studios were clearly wondering if AI could pick up work done by writers, in other words, actual scriptwriting. In fact, I used AI—coupled with human advice from a fine firm based in Ireland—to develop my book blurb.

As happened with social media and digital communication, AI is a technology shift of far-reaching proportions, still to be understood. While the "do anything" apps such as ChatGPT have received the most attention so far, many powerful apps address specific tasks: Duolingo, a language app; Grammarly, a writing assistant; and Expedia, a well-known travel app. No wonder concerns about privacy and security have quickly risen as users share data with algorithms to train the software, and the U.S. and Europe are working to draft regulations and legislation governing its use.

Amazing growth is ahead for AI, but innovations preceding the disruptive apps remain powerful—another example of the digital marketing impact of the ubiquitous smartphone. Marketers can use your phone to track your location and send relevant real-time product information while it is timely for you in your purchasing considerations. Consider what mobile technology company Didgebridge can do when you do something as simple as texting a code to a number on your iPhone.

Following a successful corporate career with major companies, John McNulty partnered with IT expert Ryan Swadley to start Didgebridge, a mobile video marketing tech company capitalizing on the trend to the Internet of Things (IoT). With the company's technology, consumers can opt in for educational marketing videos or messages on their mobile devices, so the company avoids intrusive advertising or spamming issues.

Didgebridge is riding the wave of video usage incorporated into digital marketing and social media today. Always a useful, even essential, medium for new product introductions or corporate branding, video has had explosive growth because of its ability to add drama to what can be otherwise stale texts and emails.

"The name Didgebridge was derived from digital bridge, a bridge between the old way of marketing and the new way," said McNulty. "We don't abandon the old way; we enhance it with two-way mobile video. All marketing touchpoints should be interactive and allow the consumer to engage, whether it's in TV, radio, newspaper or point of sale. We transform the old way of marketing into the new."

The value of the technology even extends to point of sale, where consumers in a store can access information about specific products that interest them in real time. The International Council of Shopping Centers reported that three-fifths of consumers prefer to be left alone to do their own things while in stores instead of engaging with real live human beings. And of course, salespeople are in short supply at most retail stores. A similar trend is happening in banking, with retail branches expected to look more like an Apple store with "consultants" assisting customers.

The Digital Age is now a mobile transformation. With more than 224 million smartphones in the USA and more than 6 billion worldwide, the transition to text and video marketing is well underway. On any given week, only about half of cell phone users actually use the phone to make a call; they are texting instead.

The mobile revolution has already proven impactful in the world of crisis communications. How many police departments have been sent reeling when a civilian shot stills or video on their cell phones of police abuse of force? The political world has had to scramble when presidential candidates such as

Hillary Clinton and Mitt Romney both made inappropriate remarks before audiences they assumed were circumspect. Not so when anyone in a group may have a smartphone activated; both were embarrassed by publication of their impolitic remarks.

Someone is watching, but it's not Big Brother; it's your neighbor, employee, stranger, or competitor.

The ability to broadcast, with or without permission, through personal media tools, must affect the third and most specific platform of communication, face-to-face communication. This is also the most credible, as it offers participants the ability to view the speaker's body language at close range and assess his or her truthfulness most directly. Televised speeches and webcasts are of course effective, low-cost means of amplifying the reach of this direct communication. Because it is so low-tech and high touch, it is probably most effective for special events such as employee meetings, sales meetings, political rallies, investor presentations, and similar venues.

TODAY, TECHNOLOGY CHANGES OUR PARADIGMS AND DRIVES OUR POLICIES

The driver of change in this new communications paradigm is undoubtedly technology. It was first evidenced by the Internet and the rush to create websites (or what we used to call "online brochures"), something of a crossbreed between the new and traditional media. Now the smartphone and the rise of social media are motivating marketers who used to create email campaigns to create text and online video campaigns.

The danger is obvious with so many mobile recording devices, but so is the opportunity to reach general or targeted audiences with positive marketing messages, warning messages in the event of a crisis, or informational messages to help in corporate recovery after a problem.

The company goal should be to recover reputation in weeks rather than, say, a year or more.

Writing these words, I took a short break to heat up a coffee pod and enjoy my favorite brew in a favorite mug. A special memento is on the kitchen shelf where we keep our coffee cups. Though inexpensive, the glass coffee mug with the circular red and blue logo of the London Underground which bears the famous motto "Mind the Gap!" is a prized souvenir. It is a reminder of that treacherous space between the station and the train car that must be navigated before one steps aboard the Tube to appreciate the wonders of a great world city.

The anonymous female voice broadcast throughout the Underground to remind tourists and citizens alike to "Mind the Gap!" is part of our fond memories, of course. And let's be frank, people need frequent reminders and updates in our busy personal and professional lives. We need to mind the gaps, as do employees and employers, because the gaps are where we fall prey to danger. They also where we find opportunities.

A landmark date in the history of corporate social media was December 17, 2008, the day the Securities & Exchange Commission made the use of interactive data, the eXtensible Business Reporting Language (XBRL), mandatory for all U.S. public companies over a three-year period. From a regulatory standpoint, the provision of interactive data and information—financial material that can be tagged, modeled, and managed by analysts—has been already mandated for U.S. companies.

The two-way feature of interactive data is of course the most attractive feature from a corporate reputation standpoint and the most vexing from the compliance and corporate governance standpoint. The term social media encompasses new ways in which new media technologies can help people communicate better and engage in a dialogue. This can be a considerably different mission than simply "managing the message." It is not necessarily contradictory, but the two goals are not necessarily the same, whether one is a CEO, a compliance officer, general counsel, or the investor relations officer. The newer online technologies have added a social and shared aspect for users so that the Internet is a two-way system.

Transparency has become the key to corporate credibility with the investing public, the consuming public, regulatory authorities, the media, and institutional investors. After all, we live in a world of very complex regulatory systems, whether companies are privately owned or publicly owned, or are considering a transition between the two. For companies considering an entry into public capital markets, whether by their own impetus or that of private equity owners, meeting the thresholds of corporate governance has become almost as great an obstacle as meeting the national exchanges' financial requirements. The use of social media by authorized company spokespeople, authorized and unauthorized employees, and third parties, is where the gap between transparency and liability becomes the clearest.

And this is true as the pace of regulation continues to grow, whether in the U.S. or overseas.

For SEC-reporting companies, the number of shareholder meetings, complying with Section 404 of Sarbanes-Oxley, and recruiting a board with a majority of independent directors are among the burdensome and costly compliance duties that must be met. Regulation FD, which imposes certain disclosure requirements on U.S.-based companies, has no such effect on foreign-owned companies. In Europe, Solvency II is another huge international regulatory scheme designed to manage risks of insurer bankruptcy. Implementation was delayed from the original 2013 implementation, but this is surely only a reprieve. The Dodd-Frank Act has imposed new regulatory costs and requirements. Banks both large and small had to consider the costs and impacts of Basel III regulation and reporting their assessment to their shareholders. While the financial impact of any one piece of regulation may in itself be moderate, in the aggregate it is costly. For example, the rapidly increased costs of compliance have prompted many small community banks to consider selling to larger banks with more ability to achieve scale.

Moreover, the communications and reporting must be transparent in a timely manner, according to accepted reporting norms. One reason is the information demands of sophisticated investors, which must be met for a company to be fairly valued in the marketplace. The other reason is simply to avoid the liabilities involved when all shareholders are not informed simultaneously of material information, or when there is employee awareness of serious misconduct. The whistleblower provisions of the Dodd-Frank Act offer attractive financial incentives for employees to call the SEC, very much along the lines of the False Claims Act, which enables whistleblowers to receive a percentage of any damages the U.S. government may recover due to reported fraud in government contracting.

Some guidelines are needed to help managers control the corporate message to meet both disclosure obligations and provide good governance while fulfilling compliance obligations. Policy development for the organization is of course a first step, both as a benchmark for progress, a planning document, and a necessary human resources and legal document. Ideas? What does policy entail? A checklist approach? Models we could hold up?

How we handle enforcement is the rub. Documenting compliance is the starting point.

Fortunately, new tools are becoming available daily to help manage these functions. For example, archiving of social media is important to document what has taken place. Like other forms of electronic communication, social media is discoverable legally, and covered by SEC and FINRA rules. FINRA Notice 10-06 and 11-39 and SEC rules 17a-3, 17a-4 and NASD rule 3110 require social media, business email, and instant messaging recordkeeping requirements. New online tools facilitate this quickly, easily, and inexpensively with cloud-based systems that capture social media activity from employees' devices, respecting user's privacy and complying with privacy laws. Simple opt-ins from users combined with usernames and passwords don't detract from the social media experience.

Social media evolves at a rapid pace. New sites and technologies appear almost monthly, changing the previous landscape overnight. This provides a company that uses social media sensitively with the opportunity to evolve with the market. And it suggests that companies who are smart adopters of corporate social media tools are most likely to be able to capitalize on broad changes in investor behavior, thus becoming more competitive in the search for capital. Even before the onset of global recession in 2008, the contraction of the sell-side made it harder and harder for micro-cap and small-cap companies to attract research attention. Companies seeking to increase visibility and improve ease of access to their information by investors will increasingly grasp that social media is a profitable channel of communication.

Economic downturns make proactive corporate information vital as investors and businesses want near real-time data on positions, pricing and risk issues. Corporate social media offers small or little-known firms another way to get attention quickly and inexpensively. Facebook® attendance for services at my small local church augments in-person attendance, with our pastor urging watchers to trigger their "likes" online. For large organizations and big companies, getting their news and information out in a structured and broader way with metrics to measure success is now the norm.

The media columnist for the *Washington Post*, Margaret Sullivan, wrote in her column, "During the Watergate era … there were three networks. Back then, what was said on those networks … was largely believed. Much more than now, there was a shared set of facts."

Fragmented media, including social media that has no editorial filter, or a very inconsistent one if users are relying on Facebook editors or AI algorithms, complicate the mission of distributing a consistent unified message considerably.

The benefits of communicating to investors with social media and interactive data are highly attractive despite the downsides that are often publicized of premature disclosures and announcements. These formats of communication allow the public (including professional investors and mutual funds as well as individual investors) to customize their view of information in the most convenient and practical way, and to cut down on information overload. In addition, many users simply may prefer interactive information to a static pdf or article.

Today social media can actually speed the corporate compliance process as well as contain costs. Compliance is the thorniest and most intimidating issue and the source of some hidden costs such as legal fees. Legal disclosures on Twitter are couched in short blurbs that can cause issues. Legal vetting of blogs authored by corporate CEOs, CFOs, or other designated spokespersons under Reg FD can be fraught with personal sensitivity, time delay, and content issues, as is true for any approved communication. This concern about liability was the single biggest issue to adoption, but cooperation among legal, human resources, and investor relations or public relations officers largely resolved these questions.

Potentially, many such questions can be answered within the context of a Reg FD stance on website disclosure as the SEC distills its position. Also, as convergence occurs, communication using social media processes can be automatically streamlined to a point where better compliance workflows are achieved. Both these factors offer improved speed and costs containment of disclosure and compliance.

Corporate social media and interactive data present challenges and opportunities, many of them self-imposed because of internal concerns and issues, sometimes due to lack of full understanding or appreciation. The time to mind these gaps and bridge them with careful preparation, planning and policies is now. And the policies must be revisited and updated on a regular basis.

INFORMATION EXPANDS AS IT'S USED

When he took off for Walden Pond more than a century ago, Henry David Thoreau complained that his peers spent too much time listening to the news. It's a good thing he's not around today.

Today we get "news" instantaneously though smartphones, mini-recorders, camcorders, email, radio, platforms such as Twitter®, Instagram®, Snapchat, Tik Tok® or Facebook®, WhatsApp®, and other private message apps, cable TV, and the Internet. So now there's an open-door policy toward all kinds of information that used to be private, ranging from the health problems of politicians to social views of celebrities.

In such a world, few facts and opinions remain secret for long. The lesson should be as clear to CEOs as it is to presidential candidates: If you have bad news to announce, better tell it all and tell it fast, or someone else will beat you to the punch.

Transparency after the fact, often coupled with a *mea culpa*, can go a long way to repairing a reputation, but the damage has been done. The CEO of Boeing promised transparency going forward after admitting to a "mistake" in handling communication of a problematic cockpit warning system involved in two Boeing 737 Max crashes that killed 346 people. The botched communication served Boeing poorly as it struggled to regain trust in product safety and quality, with international regulators reviewing software fixes before allowing the airliner to return to the skies.

Speaking at a high-profile industry venue, the Paris Air Show, Boeing head Dennis Mullenburg told reporters the company's communications with regulators, customers, and the public "was not consistent. And that's unacceptable." But he was unable to solve the operational and communications issues that bedeviled the company and was ousted by year-end. The company press release announcing his ouster said, significantly, "Under the Company's new leadership, Boeing will operate with a renewed commitment to full transparency, including effective and proactive communication with the FDA, other global regulators and its customers." As part of the transition, the company also hired a world-class communications executive who had been working with the troubled Fiat Chrysler organization.

Information that many companies used to keep "inside the family" appears routine in print and social media. Concerned shareholders are as likely to call a business reporter or email a blogger as they are to call the investor relations department; offended employees are as likely to call a lawyer as HR; and journalists are more aggressive about seeking sources of information outside official company channels.

In addition, an immense amount of material has become available through public filings with regulatory agencies. Add to that the burgeoning amount of information available in international databases, including financial and industry analyst reports that anyone with a computer can access. Just type in a few key words such as "pollution of ground water" to see which companies appear on the screen.

The information is there. And experience tells us that once it exists, it will be used.

"Information expands as it's used," noted Harlan Cleveland, professor emeritus, University of Minnesota's Hubert H. Humphrey Institute of Public Affairs. "It's transportable at the speed of light. Above all, it leaks; it has an inherent tendency to leak."

How could it not leak, given the vast amount of information available to so many individuals and groups, and the numerous low-cost, often anonymous ways to distribute the information? And these kinds of leaks can be very damaging. More than one senior executive has been shocked to see memos and planning documents quoted online leaked by disaffected employees or outsiders with access to inside information.

Of course, visibility isn't always bad. Fraud and mismanagement should be exposed. Also, valid management lessons exist in much of the material published about today's companies, with or without corporate consent. The whole process of benchmarking, for example, depends upon full, candid sharing of information. This is corporate transparency at its best.

Bottom line, managing a business with the workings

exposed even to the eyes of the competition is a challenge indeed. Business owners and managers must adapt their thinking to this environment the same way Warren Buffett has at its best—voluntary, controlled, timed, accurate, and responsible.

THE ROI OF CSR AND EGC

The moral of most of this book's stories is that you can do well by doing good.

Corporate Social Responsibility or CSR as it is known, is the catch-call phrase used to describe beneficial corporate activity beyond the profit motive. The Society of Human Resource Management defines the practice thus: "Corporate Social Responsibility represents the organization's commitment to operate in an ethical and sustainable manner by engaging in activities that promote and support philanthropy, transparency, sustainability, and ethically sound governance practices."

Perhaps the most intriguing word in the definition is transparency, a theme I've returned to again and again as the *leitmotif* for corporate values today.

Sustainability is probably the newest concept.

Originating decades ago, as the conservation movement, sustainability today refers to more than ecology and is used as shorthand for acting in a way that positive social, environmental, and economic results are achieved by an organization. The acronym for this movement, one commonly used in corporate circles, is ESG, or Environmental, Social, and Governance concerns.

More and more activist groups are raising ESG concerns through shareholder resolutions, demonstrations, or media interviews. Taken broadly, these issues can range from divesting in privately held prison companies or fossil fuel companies to the diversity and age of the board of directors. Proxy advisory firms have taken to including these issues in their ratings of publicly held companies.

Long sensitive to being activism targets, many companies have published reports on their CSR and ESG activities for decades. All too often, these have taken the form of fairly "feel good"-type reports, as there has been little quantitative information available to compare apples to apples. Most recently, an organization known as the Sustainability Accounting Standards Board, or SASB, has published measures incorporating many aspects of ESG so there can be common metrics for comparison. SASB was modeled after FASB, the Financial Accounting Standards Board, a well-respected body which for many years has published accounting rules and regulations that can be used in financial comparisons. And the SEC has moved to require disclosure of progress on climate-friendly goals.

CSR and ESG today are a clear part, and a growing part, of corporate reputation management and valuation. On the investment side, funds have been created and promoted that focus on groups of stocks that comply with good CSR and ESG practices. Many of these funds built on companies that are "doing good" have performed quite well. And as investing in this kind of company is in fact rather difficult, the funds typically charge fees which their investor have been willing, if not happy, to pay.

Clean-energy bets can take many forms, ranging from utilities to vehicle-charging systems and equipment used in water management, battery storage, solar power, and wind generation. New money has continued to pour into the field, with firms such as Neo Partners raising $800 million for a debut fund in mid-2023. Neo's founders were especially popular as they had a track record in the industry managing a clean-energy fund for Oaktree Capital, an advantage in a sector where expertise is rare.

The big question for investors considering such opportunities is: What is the additional risk? Clearly, many companies are excluded from consideration in such funds. What kind of credit and equity analysis is being done on the companies at hand? Are financial returns being sacrificed so asset managers can pick corporate winners and losers? In our polarized political environment, some states have authored legislation negating ESG investment because of "greenwashing" claims and portfolio performance concerns. It reflects real issues, as the states and their pensioners depend so heavily on the income. The ruction is: Are asset management firms and pension funds sacrificing returns to investors for the sake of virtue-signaling? This question of investment performance for climate-friendly portfolios will take years to answer, but savvy investors should be monitoring the trends and results closely.

There can be a big difference between "values investing" and the value of an investment.

4
BRANDING FOR SUCCESS

Before you can achieve, you must aspire.

Aspiring to succeed means you must change your behavior. Sometimes you need to change the behavior of colleagues, employees, and the organization with which you are associated.

There are rare individuals with the spark to be unique, with the personality that lights up a room or the vision that inspires multitudes. Steve Jobs, for example, wanted to bring easy computing power to the world at large. Michael Jordan achieved things with a basketball nobody had aspired to previously— many of them in the air! But many, in fact most of us, develop aspirations when we model our behavior after people, and we want to align ourselves with the products, services, or companies we admire.

In a word, brands.

Brands eat strategy for breakfast.

Our affection and fascination for brands is long-lasting. Why else would Americans so love to display logos across their chests on tees and hoodies, and on their ballcaps?

In 2023 no less than three major movies appeared about the birth of brands. "Flamin' Hot" told the story of a Mexican-American janitor who rose through the ranks of Frito Lay® to create the Flamin' Hot Cheetos® corn snack. "Air" memorialized the partnership between Nike® and Michael Jordan that led to Air Jordans®. "Blackberry" chronicled the rise and fall of the world's first smartphone, a defunct product still beloved.

The personal branding concept is inescapable in the news and on social media these days—well-known figures as Richard Branson, Elon Musk, or the Kardashians, for example. These individuals symbolize certain values and behaviors. That collection of attributes constitutes their brands.

Everyday people have brands too. When my friend Lynne Franklin started her own writing business known as Wordsmith after her job evaporated at a large communications agency that self-destructed, Lynne's brand focused on creating high-quality written communications for corporate senior management. Over time, her brand evolved to include public speaking at high-profile events such as TEDx®, and coaching individuals in their public speaking roles.

As Jeff Bezos, the founder of Amazon, famously said, "Your brand is what people say about you when you are not in the room."

Corporately, a brand is a product or service that performs a job for us we need done. The brand is the sum total of experiences, associations, or uses we have had with that brand, whether it be a product or a service. The Southwest Airlines brand represents on-time, safe, affordable air travel to its legions of satisfied customers. Serious damage was done to this image in December 2022 when thousands of flights were canceled within days due to tech problems on a massive scale, coping with unexpectedly large numbers of holiday fliers. Yet, by and large the company rebounded and the brand lives largely intact.

Both corporate and personal brands speak to some unique quality in the product, service, or person. In the same way that the Coke brand is more than the Coke logo, a personal brand incorporates all the qualities that give this person a distinctive mark or character.

My favorite read on the subject of global branding is a novel, not a business book. In a break from his usual science fiction themes, Williams Gibson's *Pattern Recognition* follows the adventures of a female coolhunter whose work for international consumer brands and a mysterious marketing firm crosses international borders as she becomes involved with corporate espionage and Russian oligarchs. The blurry lines between the disciplines are not as unlikely as one might think given the open world of the internet and the billions at stake with global brands and advertising. Gibson's take: The true geniuses of creating and marketing products are really people who excel at pattern recognition long before most of us.

Many companies aspire to be excellent in all they do. This lofty goal is only achieved by a few, and typically is not sustainable. For many years, Silicon Valley chipmaker Intel achieved excellence in all its operations and staff functions, from finance to marketing to manufacturing. Ultimately, volatility in its fundamental business, the tiny pieces of semiconducting material that form the basis of the integrated circuits used in electronics, affected this reputation for the worse. GE is a good example of a management paragon regarded as generally excellent, but by 2017 management transitions and a failed acquisition forced the giant company to cut 12,000 positions internationally in its power division, and to announce it was selling that division as well as others. In its annual "Management Top 250," the *Wall Street Journal* cites companies that "do everything well," a list in which the designees change almost every year.

A much more common ambition and accomplishment is to be excellent in one or several functions. Some quick examples:

Investment manager T. Rowe Price continues to excel at picking and recommending stocks to its clients even while billions of dollars pour out of the active management industry to the index funds that are cheaper to purchase and own. The firm's focus on beating the returns of the index enable it to survive and thrive even when bigger firms such as BlackRock have adopted the more popular passive asset management strategies.

In consumer finance, the company the original rewards card, Discover, would aspire to would undoubtedly be CapitalOne, which is now the category leader. CapitalOne's sterling operations and emphasis on generous, easy-to-use-anywhere reward points for its credit cards, emphasized with a long-running TV ad campaign using celebrity spokespeople ("What's in Your Wallet?"), have made it a winner. This is the company an up-and-comer would try to recruit from and study for new product development or strategy tips.

Places can be brands too. A large part of the London brand is its long-standing presence as the financial capital of Europe. Yet, increasingly, young traders and software coders are shunning London for the lure of Luxembourg or other cities where youth and the startup culture is prized, and the imbroglio of Brexit is a non-factor.

Cities such as San Francisco, Austin and Portland enjoyed the brand of being hip, cool, safe places in which to live and work. By 2023 they had become known as dirty, high-crime, high-tax places in which to live and work, with corresponding exits of citizens and businesses.

For many of us, the personal, professional, and corporate may well blend. When Mark Rosenbloom bought a mid-size office building in north suburban Chicago, he installed what he called "Inspire TV" in the building lobby. He hired a Hollywood producer to create a movie theater-quality projector and screen arrangement that displayed positive quotes and images with upbeat music. The display ranges from Louis Armstrong music with quotes from people such as Albert Einstein to the Yoda quote from *Star Wars*: "Do or do not, there is no try." Rosenbloom explained that he simply wanted people entering the building "to feel happier about their work and their lives" while differentiating his building from others in a crowded local office marketplace.

Hedge funds, the privately organized investment vehicles known for their secrecy, are typically not recognized for being worker-friendly or supportive of the career goals of women and other minorities.

When Ray Dalio, the founder of one of the world's largest hedge funds, Bridgewater Associates, received negative feedback from employees about their treatment, he was genuinely surprised at the negative opinions. Moving beyond his own quite natural defensive reactions, he acted within the firm to address the issues and improve the company culture. An internal guidebook he created called *Principles* became a hallmark of the firm and so well-known within the industry, it was eventually published as a hardbound book for the general public.

By this point in your reading here, it should almost go without saying that real brands are transparent. In other words, they are honest—but not always necessarily consistent.

Anything fake will quickly become apparent in today's full-disclosure society. That will quickly lead to loss of reputation, lost sales, and lost customer relationships.

Beyond mainstream brands, there are also niche brands or cult brands—brands that a small minority of people identify with and seek to own. Harley-Davidson motorcycles were once a cult brand and are today a mainstream brand that has moved far beyond the outlaw image that originally sparked its fame. More on this phenomenon in a moment.

Right-hand brands are the ones we turn to automatically, by default, when we are shopping in a certain category—say, Harry's for shaving, or Honda for automobiles. Aspirational brands are ones we would like to own but for economic reasons probably can't—a Rolex watch, for example, or a Cartier handbag. The world's richest person sits atop the LVMH luxury empire with brands including Christian Dior, Tag Heuer watches, Louis Vuitton, and Tiffany. The brands have done so well in the turbulent post-COVID lockdown economy that Paris headquarters became a target for street protests after French President Macron's plan to raise the national retirement age from 62 to 64 sparked ongoing demonstrations.

In recent years the concept of personal brands has become in vogue, and it is a useful way to think of marketing and growing ourselves. Most people you think of who have one-word names are brands—Hillary, Bernie, Sting, Shaq, Oprah, Madonna. When we hear the name, we know immediately who they are and whether or not they appeal to us.

For the sake of convenience, I used to refer to all the brands referenced above as wonder brands. Okay, partly because, we all wonder how they became so successful! But mainly, it's because these brands have *achieved* something wonderful. But the truth behind a strong brand is that it is really *a powerhouse*. It may not appeal to you personally, but its strength is undeniable.

The word powerhouse is itself full of attraction. A Washington power broker once moved his consulting firm's headquarters to a building that once was the electrical powerhouse for downtown Washington, D.C. The halo effect of being at "the powerhouse" was itself part of the founder's brand.

And in the wake of attractive powerhouse personal brands, millions seek to play golf like Tiger Woods (or use the golf clubs he may endorse or the courses he may play), sport the dress worn by Michelle Obama or the watch worn by David Beckham, or vacation at the spot frequented by movie stars.

THE CULT OF BRAND PERSONALITY

For sake of convenience in beginning this discussion, I've highlighted many well-known brands; however, you don't need to be an international giant to benefit from the impact of brands. Quite the contrary, branding can be felt all around you, wherever you may live. After all, most small businesses have under $250,000 in sales and are local in nature. The dry cleaner that has accurate, on-time delivery. The local grocery store that offers cooking classes and can be seen at local farmer's markets offering locally grown products. The neighborhood coffee shop with college kids for baristas with a roasted coffee flavor you love—and, hey, it just contracted with a local microbrewery to use its coffee in brewing a dark beer, expanding the reach and sales of both businesses. The car dealership with its emphasis on quick-lane service and generosity with loaner cars. The icecream store whose name is on all the jerseys of the kids' sports teams.

Each of these young (or mature) businesses has created a

platform for growth and generated loyal customers by adopting a branding strategy.

Growing a business around a core group of loyal buyers is a powerful strategy to compete against companies with larger advertising and marketing budgets, or to distinguish yourself in a crowded market. This is the appeal of cult brands to savvy marketers and business owners everywhere.

Cult brands are niche products that attract a loyal following few mainstream brands enjoy. By employing a cult brand strategy, managers working with a struggling brand suddenly can be sitting on top of a gold mine. For those few managers of power brands dominating a product category or a given geography, a cult brand could be their fiercest competitor—or their next acquisition.

What sets a cult brand apart from brands that attract loyalty or have positive brand images is the passion they arouse in the customer. Any brand, just like any person, has a personality. Yet not every person has a passionate following.

Nor does every brand. Cult brands have charisma that is off the charts. The customer and the brand have a relationship, an affinity without a rationale, often an emotional rather than an intellectual response.

Owners and managers interested in building a cult brand have an attractive opportunity to grow market share rapidly. Profits are likely to follow, as purchasers of cult brands are typically willing to pay premium prices to obtain the products they love.

Far from being an obstacle, scarcity may even enhance the appeal of the product or service. Witness the example of Harley-Davidson motorcycles. Not only are they premium-priced; at one point, purchasers were in line for up to two years to buy a new one (this was well before the COVID-19 global pandemic contributed to widespread shortages in parts and goods). Food items, craft beers, and pet veterinary and grooming services are other examples.

Often it seems that products attain cult status for no reason other than the cultural whims and faddism. However, more careful study shows there are some common denominators. Here are three suggestions on how to assess the reputational appeal of a brand and go about creating a cult following:

Know what's precious about the brand and protect it. Imagine if Maker's Mark® bourbon started selling its high-quality product in containers other than distinctive bottles with the red wax seal. The product that is consumed would retain its legendary quality, but would it maintain the mystique that made it popular? Personally, I think Corona® beer made a huge mistake in adding cans to its line-up beyond its distinctive bottles. The product may be the same, but it's lost that distinctive *je ne sais quoi,* and while gaining sales, the brand has certainly lost fervid fans. Managing the magnetism of a brand is a tricky assignment.

Think in terms of creating a club rather than building market share. In traditional marketing, the measure of success is share of market. With cult brands the growth driver is repeat business from the core group of loyal customers. By definition, the cult brand will not be No. 1 in its market.

The mindset of starting a club has important implications for the marketer. Building a database of customers and prospects for targeting mailings is critical. Many self-published authors know this tactic: they provide free books and other incentives to attract prospective readers to their newsletters—and then they offer exclusive content to retain their subscribers. Customer referral programs, in which existing customers receive an incentive for referring new customers, are logical outgrowths. PR image-building programs and special event marketing also can play critical roles.

Sell to fans or club members rather than customers. Think of the Harley-Davidson® rides in which hundreds of owners take their choppers out for a long weekend trip. While Harley has grown dramatically over the years and even added an affiliated, less expensive brand, it's not built markets in the traditional sense; it's formed clubs of dedicated buyers. Its hometown of Milwaukee is well-accustomed to seeing locals drive experimental Harleys around town, and there's a museum to the local icon there as well as its factory.

Look at things from the perspective of a small, defined group. We need to be able to say, "There's some attitude or aspiration there that we can reach on a deep level." The marketer is making an appeal that will have a very emotional, intense response.

This requires a deep understanding of consumers (your club members!) and their motivations. Marketing firms with skilled in-house researchers and marketing agencies with brand planners may have much to offer in pursuing this strategy. And so can a company founder who's simply set out to solve a problem.

Don't follow the rules; cult marketing is a strategy for risk takers. In many cases, especially when using social media, the strategies and tactics used by cult marketers cannot be truly tested in advance. Regular reach and frequency numbers don't apply. Instead, the message may be: We're all part of one big family— and wouldn't you like to be part of that family too?

A major issue for marketers is how broadly a core group of buyers can expand before the brand begins to lose its cult mystique. A working hypothesis says that many brands have the potential to build a large mainstream following while holding onto the original following. If this is true, it provides an evolving way to look at brand loyalty and marketing.

Ben & Jerry's® ice cream is a good example. To people who aren't dedicated to wearing Ben & Jerry's T-shirts or saving the rain forest, it's just darn good ice cream. Nike also has a strong cult following dating from the very founding of the company, based on shoe technology, athletic performance, and celebrity endorsers. But a lot of people just buy Nikes because they are good shoes.

No question, it's tougher for some brands and categories than it is for others to build a core group of dedicated buyers. Striving for a distinctive reputation is difficult, and once a brand has it, it's possible, even easy, to lose it. However, the strategy opens up some rare and exciting growth opportunities.

5
FAMILY TIES

Jim Boccarosso, who had founded and sold three companies, was dating a successful career woman who left her job to follow her vision of creating a company. Her concept for the aerospace company that became Air Spares Unlimited was to focus on making, sourcing, and repairing landing gears, wheels and brakes. However, her expertise was primarily in sales and marketing. Jim was so impressed with her ideas that he volunteered to help scale the business and serve as CEO.

Stephanie has a little different take on this creation story. "I couldn't afford to hire a CEO," she says, "so I married one."

Today the husband-and-wife entrepreneurs have a rapidly growing business with family and friends at the core. Many of the best employees and business service providers came to them through referrals within their closely knit group. As new parents, the couple are including a nanny center in the company's headquarters office so they and others can keep their young children close.

With sales growing rapidly, talent acquisition has been a

major focus. They pay a premium for quality space on Chicago's famous Michigan Avenue, a location that attracts the kind of quality, younger workforce other companies are also vying for, people who want to live and work in a vibrant downtown rather than undertake a difficult suburban slog each day.

In a first for Jim, the company is self-funding. His previous startups relied on venture capital or other outside sources of funding. And an exit strategy? Not even in the cards yet, as everyone focuses on sales and building an innovative company in a very specific market sector.

It's hard to estimate how many couples are working together in the same entrepreneurial business, but anecdotal evidence suggests the number is growing. Lifestyle choices, the availability of ready capital, the global pandemic, and a more independent spirit among younger professionals is driving the trend. These individuals have often, too, seen their Baby Boomer parents ousted unceremoniously from highly paid jobs that are difficult to replace. They have not necessarily bought into the appeal or status of working for large corporations but are often willing to work for companies of which the average person has never heard. It's quite possible that many of these young companies will eventually be true family-owned enterprises.

In the popular mind, of course, family businesses are enterprises where the ownership is passed down from generation to generation. This model is under pressure, and the future is likely to see more of these companies sold to peers, outsiders, or private equity investors.

Family-owned companies and closely held companies are not necessarily the same. Closely held companies typically only have two or three owners. This may be true of a family-owned company, but there may be only one owner (the founder) or there may be many.

Either type of business may have distinctive issues rather capital or selling itself. Sometimes the lines are actually blurred. Generally, if an investor is putting in less than 50% of the ownership capital, this would be considered a financing, but if they are putting in more, it may well be regarded as a transaction (i.e., a purchase or M&A deal). Status as a transaction means investment bankers or other middlemen would charge higher fees, and also obviously has significant legal considerations.

Other matters may often arise, sometimes at the last minute. It is easy to forget the importance of real estate (either owned or leased), which in closely held corporations may not be held by the entire ownership group. This means a separate negotiation may be needed, both with the buyers or financiers, and sometimes with the investment bankers (most of whom would not hold a commercial real estate license and thus would not be experts in the matters at hand).

Buying and selling family-owned companies presents its own unique set of challenges. One of the threshold issues is simply placing a value on the company. Publicly held companies have shares, the price of which can be tracked in real time 24-7, and a wealth of legally required information that is available to all. Closely held and family companies are harder to value by definition, with shares that may be illiquid and owners who may have unrealistic expectations.

Jeff Temple, CEO of a mid-market investment bank with 30 professionals, Peakstone, notes that this size of company is often not experienced in M&A. "Family and owner-owned or closely held businesses often fail to understand the range of options a business owner has—including shareholders of closely held businesses. They very frequently do not understand what their options are or have misunderstandings of what their options are."

Some of the contributions of advisors can be basic but critical. In the case of one consumer business, the owner had been using a family law practitioner unaccustomed to commercial transactions. Ultimately, the owner revised the purchase agreement without counsel and sent it to the buyer—but without informing the buyer that revisions to the document had been made! That of course ended the negotiation.

Sometimes the buyer completes the sale, results turn down, and the buyer immediately contemplates lawsuits against the seller and his investment bank. Well-written contracts can typically deter this from actually happening.

Many an investment banker or business broker has lamented that they were close to placing a company on the market just when it lost a major client, revenues fell short of goal, or the EBITDA number sank. Nobody wants to buy a rapidly melting ice cube.

Usually, bad news puts the deal on hold. Or it craters. Sometimes, however, owners proceed with the sale process, realizing the gain they will achieve will be less than originally anticipated. A lot depends on the seller's personal financial situation and pain threshold.

In one case, a manufacturing company that had been listed for sale for almost a year attracted a prospective buyer, but during due diligence, an EPA concern was found. The asset purchase agreement was revised to include a remediation issue, which the buyer was willing to pay for. Later, a worker compensation issue emerged. The asset purchase agreement was revised again. At this point the seller was becoming impatient, and simply abandoned the plan to sell.

Conversely, when valuations are high, deal making can be

low. This is especially true when buyers are weighing the risks of the transaction. Life sciences IPOs were at a highpoint in 2015 with 74 recorded, falling somewhat to 63 by 2018, but M&A activity was minimal. As valuations reset by 2019, deal making was on the uptick. Especially in sectors such as life sciences or technology, acquisition is a classic strategy for obtaining intellectual property and technology.

The more critical issues, however, relating to this last point, are often the intangibles of the family's group dynamics.

Numerous family factors, including cultural issues as well as family-specific issues, may factor in. The checklist includes:

- Grandparents, parents, children, grandchildren
- Divorce
- No children
- Siblings
  - Competition, rivalry
  - Working styles
  - Future generations (succession)
- In-laws
- Non-family members
  - Board. Independent members?
  - Management. Third-party professionals?
  - Advisors

Jeff Temple notes that a typical transaction in his process can take six to eight months to close, which is relatively quick. However, the process of due diligence, the investigation of a business conducted by the buyer and his advisors, can be quite off-putting in and of itself. "The process is incredibly invasive. Business owners don't see the context of that. Business owners need to be prepared to divulge anything and everything about their business. Buyers are incredibly sophisticated, there's no hiding any flaws in the business, and they must be prepared to be as transparent as possible."

Even the smallest business, a so-called "mom and pop" with sales under $1 million, must be prepared for the process. The more that is done in advance, the better. Three years of financials. Lists of contracted customers. Pro forma financials. Reputable advisors will have checklists to help the business owner prepare.

"Business owners, especially successful entrepreneurs, have very strong, very emotional attachments to their businesses," says Jeff Temple. "They are optimistic by nature and are not prepared for someone to come in looking for warts, poking holes, skeptical of every projection. Plenty of deals fall apart for reasons that are emotional and not business related. An advisor who's neutral can be the difference between a deal closing and a deal that falls apart."

Steve Eschbach echoes this sentiment. "In bringing a trusted advisor into the arena, you pay more in hourly fees, but there will be fewer hours than a poorly trained professional and you see more value."

One point I've often made to both buyers and sellers is to think beyond the actual valuation performed by an outside expert and to try to consider the value of the combined company. That requires some imaginative thinking, and probably the assumption of more risk.

At some point in every family, wealth generation gives way to the pressure for wealth preservation. What happens when there is no younger family member trained and poised to assume ownership and leadership as the older generation seeks to retire or to become liquid?

A 2019 survey of Midwestern manufacturing companies by a

trade association found that half of the companies whose owners were over 55 had no plans for succession.

"This is a crisis for the manufacturing sector," said Dan Swinney, executive director of Manufacturing Renaissance, the group that conducted the survey. "This whole sector of the economy is left up to the whims and contradictions inside individual families."

Many companies, and in fact whole industries such as community banking or metalworking, fall victim to what I call "board fatigue." Family members in their 70s simply become worn out with the rigors of the public markets or managing a business after decades of up-and-down business cycles. While board memberships can be highly sought after, finding qualified minority directors, or individuals willing to bear the legal liability of the position (especially in the audit committee), can be daunting. In fact, identification of candidates to join the boards of smaller companies or geographically undesirable companies can be nearly impossible.

Yet there are success stories. Typically, we think of family owned companies as small businesses. That is in fact the norm. The foundry or metal casting industry, for example, has 1,900 members, most of them family owned companies employing fewer than 50 people with annual sales of $5 million or less.

On the other hand, consider that up to 33% of the Fortune 500 are companies that got their start as family ventures, and more than 40% were founded by immigrants or their children.

Not quite in the league of the Fortune 500—yet—is one example of a large Midwestern bank that started a family-owned community bank, then went public, with the family retaining board seats and a large percentage of the outstanding shares. Wisely, they hired an outside president and CEO with banking experience to help drive growth and quality.

MidWestOne Financial Group is based in Iowa City, Iowa, a healthy market with a large state university, good infrastructure and a good location. Iowa, however, is a low-growth market. Many Iowa towns today still have the same population they had in the 1950s. Charlie Funk, a long-time community banker hired as the first CEO outside of family, recognized the need for acquisition as well as internal, organic growth. With family and board approval he drove several large acquisitions that increased the bank's capital from $1 billion to more than $5 billion. The bank also made smaller deals to enter new geographic markets such as Denver or to enter new industry sectors. His strategy was to supplement the large acquisitions by hiring small groups of bankers looking to re-affiliate.

As Charlie tells it, "The company was founded by Ben Summerwill in 1934. Until 2008, the company was privately held and the Summerwill family controlled 55% of the stock outstanding. A 2008 merger of equals doubled the size of the company, made us a public company traded on the NASDAQ, and the family interest was reduced to about 31%. Since that time, there have been two other rather sizable acquisitions. Although family members have sold relatively few shares over the years, the percentage of ownership will fall to roughly 20% when the most recent acquisition closes."

What is the key to balancing the needs of shareholders, employees and family members without shortchanging any of them? "Only one member of the Summerwill family serves on the board and there are no members of the family in company management. The family member currently serving on the board is one of our best directors and a leader within the board. Family members remain interested in the company, but do not weigh in frequently with their opinions. They rely on the corporate dividend; should there be a negative change in the payout, the decibel level likely would rise! It is also worthy to note that the patriarch and former CEO of the family is 84 and still attends board members as an advisory member."

As with other CEOs interviewed for this book, size does matter, he opines, for the company to meet the needs of all stakeholders and prosper as an independent organization. "Similar to other industries, banking has a trend toward acquiring more scale to be successful. Scale does not automatically guarantee success, but it helps. The 2015 acquisition made us a multi-state institution and represented a milestone of sorts in the evolution of the company. While the acquisition was bumpy and integration issues lasted longer than they probably should have, there is no question that the move was a good one for the future of the company. The pending acquisition will move us near the $5 billion asset mark and the acquisition is expected to be less complicated than in 2015-16. As we have grown and gained more institutional shareholders, financial returns are elevated in importance and visibility. When we were a privately held company, the family did expect competitive returns, but with 45% of shareholders institutional, the for-profit element is simply more visible. The challenge is to retain the good parts of family and community banking and talk about them frequently."

With a good thing going, there are no plans to sell. "The current plans are to remain independent and growth prudently. What the board and management understand is that we earn our independence, so financial returns must be competitive. The attractiveness of our company as an acquisition target does appear to be good at this time, but there are no plans to sell for the foreseeable future."

The truly wealthy families—those who own sports league franchises or inherit furniture store or real-estate empires and the like—employ wholly owned or contracted service firms called family offices to guide and manage their investments. For many, the family office role has expanded to include all manner of personal services, such as buying and selling homes, transportation, advice on art investments—basically, anything a truly wealthy person may need.

The industry trade group, the Family Office Association, says it "creates value for families and their family offices to grow wealth, strengthen legacy, and unite multiple generations." A senior officer at Morgan Stanley PWM, which caters to families whose wealth stretches across generations, put it this way: "Our job is to protect our client's lifestyle. [That] means considerably more to the family than beating the S&P 500 Index." Which makes sense for the families at the highest economic echelons.

The investment groups of even large family offices tend to be small—only two or three people—so when they are engaged in due diligence on a potential transaction, they may be out-of-pocket for an entire quarter or more. This little-understood fact probably accounts for the frustration many young companies or public companies reaching out to them may feel, as they are somewhat opaque by design. Family offices tend to be clubby, which actually is a strength, as they network among themselves for insights on industries and operations. They are difficult to find and contact. That said, they can be attractive investors. They are constantly on the hunt for "the next Starbucks" or its ilk, and tend to be patient, friendly investors with many connections to offer.

And their approaches continue to evolve. Five years ago, most family offices of any size were seeking to buy into private equity syndicates that held 10 companies or more. Today they are much more interested in one-offs, especially unique one-offs. And like everyone else, they appreciate quicker returns.

For those seeking only injections of capital, there also are available individual "angel" investors and, if they can be identified, loose confederations of investors willing to pool capital to invest profitably. An advantage to retaining qualified advisors is that they often have access to such networks. Even so, there are still no guarantees. It's important to be realistic with an honest assessment of the credit quality of a buyer; many aspiring entrepreneurs may well need to tap a home equity line of credit or seek contributions from friends and family. Bank financing is difficult, as they are most likely to lend based on the revenue reported to the IRS. In a business with heavy cash at the point of sale—restaurants, dry cleaners, coffee shops, and so on—documenting the cash revenue for purposes of securing a bank loan can be problematic.

In fact, even securing advisors can be difficult. A number of business brokers note that a seller willing to provide an upfront cash stake, which would be deducted at the time of sale, gets their attention quickly, as this is an indication the seller is serious. There is obviously much higher risk to the advisor for an all-commission agreement, which is why many investment banks insist on a monthly retainer.

All advisors, from Peakstone's Temple to Transworld's Eschbach, stress the importance of an advisor in opening up possibilities that business buyers and sellers may never have considered. "We help owners find confidential solutions," says Eschbach. "Everything doesn't have to be a sale, but there does have to be a solution."

6

UNICORNS, BULLS AND BEARS

Is it possible to brand yourself for financial success? Or build a corporate brand that creates wealth in the public stock markets or among private investors?

The good news is, yes.

Of course, if it was easy, everybody would do it.

Start with the idea that there's more than one way to make money.

"The general who wins the battle makes many calculations before the battle is fought," said the master strategist of the sixth century, Sun Tzu, who is much beloved by corporate strategists today. For corporate leaders looking to raise capital or go public in the 21st century, not much has changed—success depends on planning and a strong team. In today's rapidly changing, technology-based world, one of us can't know everything, but all of us can.

At one time, it was the aspiration of every company to go public. There are still solid reasons for principals to consider this option. The principals go from private holdings to stock ownership on a listed exchange, with typically only 20-30% of the company being sold to the public. The principals keep most of the ownership, rather than giving control away as in most private equity or venture capital transactions, and they can liquidate their positions at a later date. Of course, insiders and valued employees benefit hugely from the uptick in share price once the IPO (Initial Public Offering) is accomplished.

Also, it is a commonly held viewpoint that publicly held companies are of higher quality than privately held companies as they are subject to greater regulation from a stock exchange and the Securities & Exchange Commission (SEC). They are presumed to be larger than privately held companies and are easier to value because of the existence of shares circulating in a liquid market. Wall Street is full of positive followers of a stock and the public markets (the bulls) and as well as those who are more negative (the bears).

This model no longer holds true to such a clear extent. A third animal grouping needs to be considered, the unicorns. Unicorns are privately held companies with a valuation of $1 billion or more. Being identified as a unicorn, or as a public company that is followed by bulls and bears, is itself a moniker that contributes to brand presence. The growth of a large investment market in privately held companies has been a huge boon to their growth and reduces the need to go public in many cases.

There are more than 200 such companies with total valuation estimated as high as $1.3 trillion by the *VentureBeat* data source. Notable lists of unicorn companies are maintained by *The Wall Street Journal*, *Fortune* Magazine, TechCrunch, and many other sources. The lists have included such notable companies as ride-sharing ventures Uber® and Lyft®, coworking space WeWork®, streaming TV and movie service Hulu, software maker Palantir, and the pioneer in electronic signature technology, DocuSign, several of which have since gone public, not all successfully. WeWork became a "busted IPO" when financial skeptics steered clear of the company's business model and management quality despite its operations continuing to be fairly healthy.

In a survey of 1,600 early-stage startup founders by startup accelerator Techstars, just 16% of respondents said their primary goal was to go public, compared with 28% that wanted to stay private and 36% that wanted to be acquired by a large corporate buyer. Of course, when the economy recovers and valuations pick up, these numbers may change quickly.

When private, these companies do not incur the cost of being a public company filed with the SEC or the listing costs of an exchange and accompanying compliance and regulatory costs. These fees, some of which are based on market capitalization, can run into the hundreds of thousands of dollars or more. Moreover, the unicorns are typically regarded as being of the same quality as peer companies would be in the public markets. By and large, the unicorns, because of their size and ability to afford internal staffs and the high-quality advisors, are in a position to create a well-known brand and provide for growth. While doing business as privately held companies, they have the internal resources and capable outside advisors that enable them to effectively function with the financial controls and operational savvy of their publicly held brethren. This is not an inconsiderable advantage.

Venture capitalists, private equity firms and private investors, as well as employees and owners, have profited handsomely when exiting unicorn investments such as Dollar Shave Club, eyeglass provider Warby Parker or bootmaker Ugg. Their exit can be through a sale of the company or an IPO. The decision is usually dictated by market conditions.

Not all such exits have been successful—the well-publicized

disappointments when unicorns Snap and Blue Apron went public in early 2017 dampened the entire market at the time—but there is always a long list of quality companies considering going public. The appeal goes beyond the need for capital which is omnipresent. The excitement of the process and of having your own stock ticker symbol is an unbeatable lure for founders and early investors. So is the thrill of potential price increases once the stock starts trading.

The IPO market reached a high in terms of stock market valuations and quality and quantity of IPOs in 2014, declined considerably for the following several years, and seems poised to take off again in 2018 in beyond thanks to tax reform legislation and less-restrictive government legislation. Biotech companies and fintechs (financial technology firms that unbundled and digitized many products offered by traditional lenders) accounted for much of the growth that did occur. Such creative industries demonstrate why a healthy IPO market is so important to the U.S. economy. Large tech IPOs created a wave that shaped up to make 2019 a banner year for IPOs. The market newsletter *Stock Analysis* summarized the situation neatly by pointing out there was a record number in 2021 of 1,035 IPOs, up dramatically from the previous year's total of 480. Since then the market has waned due to inflation, rising interest rates and the war in Ukraine affecting investor sentiment and valuations; 2022 and 2023 saw few IPOS come to market. In 2023 the small numbers that did well were mainly carve-outs from larger companies that were sold in the public markets.

Higher stock market valuations certainly should encourage more unicorns and small companies to undertake the rigors of the public markets. The unicorns enjoy the advantage of being able to access the capital markets fairly readily. Many of their owners were savvy enough to realize that when the door was open to obtain funding, they should rush through it. A 2018 analysis by the *Wall Street Journal* found that private capital markets "more than doubled in size over the past decade, surpassing the growth of public stocks and bonds available to all investors. At least $2.4 trillion was raised privately in the U.S. last year [2017]."

With layoffs affecting technology talent, volatile capital markets and higher interest rates, scaring up new capital for young companies became much harder by the third quarter of 2022. Seed investments in the U.S. dropped 40% from a year earlier to $3.1 billion, invested through 829 deals, a 50% decline, according to PitchBook-NCVA Venture Monitor.

THE QUEST FOR CAPITAL

Sadly, many small business owners only try to find capital when they are hard-pressed and really need it. This puts them at a disadvantage; raising money takes time unless investors are standing by in the wings (a rarity) or there are family and friends available with ready cash. Nor can one presume there are interested third-party investors willing to risk their capital without expecting a high return, a quick return or a significant ownership position in the business.

This short-sightedness is due to several factors. One, owners have a business to run. They are busy and focused on making sales, hiring, and overseeing operations. Therefore, point two, asking for money is likely to be a task they have relatively little time to do, and it is a chore they are uncomfortable undertaking. My experience with business owners and senior executives is that they tend to avoid the tasks they dislike, or do a poor job. Ironically, they also are the people most qualified to do it: No one understands a business better than the owner, and the owner is often the chief salesperson of his products or services.

John McNulty, CEO of tech startup Didgebridge, is also fundraiser-in-chief, reaching out to logical business partners as well the usual funding sources. "As we have evolved, we have been able to attract a considerable amount of capital," McNulty told us. "It came from strategic angel investors, savvy people who own their own business. They can bring us clients, and we can help them with our services. We have also cultivated relationships with strategic partners, including one very large technology company that is collaborating with us and someday would be a very logical exit candidate for us."

All too often, the owner has no trusted advisor to turn to in the arcane art of raising money. This can come back to hurt you in many ways. More on this later.

Surprisingly, expertise in corporate finance or capital markets can be scarce at the board level for smaller companies. When Adam J. Epstein was co-manager of a special situations hedge fund, his firm met with more than 1,000 small-cap companies and found that fewer than 10% of the boards had internal capital markets expertise. This is a flaw that leads many companies to do bad financings.

No surprise. Many of the institutions investing in young companies, startups or IPOs are often small hedge funds. Firms with under $100 million in assets under management have very few reporting responsibilities, so their operations and investments can be opaque. Again, advisors who know the space and know the players are essential. Who really has money to invest, and who really is a potential long-term investor? After all, the rationale for a hedge fund and its high fees (traditionally 2% of assets plus 20% of any profits, the famous "2 and 20" formula) —returns to the investor that are significantly above those most people can enjoy—disappears if the hedge fund under-performs.

A toxic financing can mean the death of a company. Paying too much for capital may force an owner to sell his creation in whole or in part. It may crimp growth down the road by restricting options to sell, expand or attract new partners. As mentioned previously, financing that includes a change of control in the business may well be viewed as a merger-and-acquisition activity by investment banks, commercial banks and lawyers, requiring an entirely different fee structure and set of legal documents—a pricey mistake. Also, some financiers play the hardest game of hardball you can imagine. SoftBank founder Masayoshi Son, a legendary investor, has been known to push tech startups to accept his money, or he will fund a rival. This strategy enabled him to garner a 15% stake in ride provider Uber that he otherwise would not have obtained.

The answer to avoiding this set of problems, in short, is to put in place a good team likely to include financial and accounting advice, investor relations and public relations assistance to build the brand and create awareness, and legal assistance. Financial expertise may well include an investment bank if not a commercial bank. There are plenty of investment banks willing to take on small companies if they are promised work (for example, with syndication of stock, takeover defense, capital raising, finding investors, public offerings, or M&A trans-actions). While retaining trusted advisors may look expensive to a small company, selecting the right advisor can save huge sums both short-term and long-term, and often can provide a huge upside in the value of the business.

Capital raising can be especially frustrating for very small companies. VentureDNA, a boutique advisory firm which keeps a low profile, receives 100-150 inquiries a year and culls this list down to about three active engagements per year. The vetting procedure includes a series of personal meetings, phone calls and due diligence activity. A pipeline of sales and strong management pedigrees will tend to quickly interest founder Stewart Dixon, who says "seventy percent of the decision is based on the people."

His firm backed a data center, for example, that owns and operates a facility offering colocation, private cloud, and electro-magnetic pulse (EMP) protection services, primarily to small and middle-market companies. A female entrepreneur was launching a women's health beverage available at retail. Another company offers Infrastructure-as-a-Service (Iaas), designed to modernize government agency payment applications and data management.

These companies rely on Dixon and his colleagues to provide advisory services in marketing and financing. They also want to access to his network of family offices and capital groups. "We are a coach with a whistle," Dixon likes to say. By focusing on a small number of companies with top talent, everyone gets personal attention. "We work alongside the entrepreneur by helping grow his business. We are embedded in the company, and in fact one client has one of our colleagues on staff as an employee. He may stay with them after the Series A or come back to us. I look at VentureDNA as a platform of opportunity, not only for entrepreneurs but for CEOs or other executives who may have exited a company and are looking to do something different."

VentureDNA is what is known in the industry as an independent sponsor, something of a boutique private equity firm. Its clients are too small to qualify for Series A round of financing, the first level of financing for a business after its initial seed capital. Dixon's assignment is typically to aid the firm in getting to the Series A round. The Series A round may range from $1.5 million to $3-4 million in many cases. While helping to raise funds, the funds actually go straight to the company rather than through VentureDNA. Dixon's firm is compensated in fees, much like a law firm or accounting firm. Should the need arrive for a firm with a FINRA license to buy or sell shares in a later round of financing, Dixon partners with an investment bank.

Unlike many firms in the finance area, Dixon and his associates keep a low social-media profile, as do some other smaller power players such as Roundtable Healthcare Partners, also based in the tony suburb of Lake Forest, 40 miles north of Chicago. Such firms can generate results for owners just as well as their larger brethren. It depends upon owner expectations and capabilities, industry sector, the chemistry between owner and adviser, and, most importantly, client company performance.

Some banks, such as the mid-market Peakstone Group, are sector-agnostic and accustomed to working with entrepreneurs in many industry categories. At one point, Peakstone was engaged to work with a short-line railroad operator on the East Coast, United Rail, to arrange approximately $10 million of funding for the acquisition of additional short-line rail operations. This type of series of deals, a "roll-up" in industry parlance, enabled the company to source new customers and improve efficiency through a pipeline of additional short-line targets, all railroads that provide passenger excursions and freight rail operations. Peakstone's initial fund raise generated a very healthy response of 52 NDAs (Non-Disclosure Agreements indicating interest and agreeing to confidentiality). Peakstone also advised a Midwestern multi-location collision repair operator, Crash Champions LLC, in connection with a capital raise, and helped sell a $15 million dollar, 40-year-old non-union trucking company on its sale. So, while Big Tech may garner many media headlines, there is a healthy amount of action with more traditional and even mature industrial and service companies.

Sometimes the numbers must be much bigger to bring a product to market, especially in the consumer world. The same bank, working with an early-stage consumer products company seeking debt or equity capital to launch a direct-to-consumer disruptive shaving product, needed to build on the $30 million of equity capital it had already raised. The opportunity in the men's direct-to-consumer market had already been demonstrated by the success of Harry's (now sold at Target and Wal-Mart as well) and the Dollar Shave Club. But the potential is even greater: Consumer testing of the company's grooming product and direct-to-consumer delivery model demonstrated the possibility of creating a global brand with more than $500 million in annual revenue.

For those interested in exploring the complicated world of initial public offerings, the next chapter goes into much more detail.

7

THE ABCS OF IPOS

For corporate issuers considering going public, going it alone is never a good strategy. It is worthwhile to begin a relationship with qualified investment banks, accountants, lawyers, and investor relations experts well in advance. Selecting an advisor with good references, including personal referrals if possible, who has the right expertise, and with whom the business owner is comfortable, is all-important.

I learned this to my regret when advising a large privately held software company that was seeking to go public. The company management wanted to use its own law firm to oversee the IPO even though the law firm had never helped take a company public. Bad idea. Within a month, it was clear the firm's attorneys were in way over their heads. The firm had to be replaced on the project with a law firm experienced in IPOs. This was a black eye for the management team to the board of directors, and in fact, the board required a review of all other advisors as well to determine their suitability, including their investment banks and IR counsel—namely, me! This delay set back the progress of the IPO procedure, and at a fairly sensitive point in time, threatening to derail the entire event.

These best practices need to be undertaken regardless of whether or not a company is proceeding to go public under the provisions of the Jumpstart Our Business Startups Act of 2012, known as The JOBS Act. This legislation was designed to fast track the IPO process for emerging growth companies, or EGCs, from a regulatory standpoint. These smaller IPOs are often called "JOBS Act IPOs" or "Reg A+" deals in reference to the law that spawned them. However, all companies need to consider the markets for their stock, and their obligations once they are publicly traded.

TRANSPARENCY BUILDS TRUST

Transparency is at the heart of all these investor communications. The need for communication is actually paramount for a JOBS Act IPO, as it may be done without an investment banker in some cases and requires only two years of audits; the company stock may struggle for visibility or credibility without support. Also, the strategy proved ideal for community banks trying to raise reserve capital, and of course banking is a very conservative industry category with many cautious investors.

The JOBS Act IPO was considered highly experimental at the time, but its creativity was exceeded with the rise of the bitcoin world and the ICO, or Initial Coin (or Currency) Offering. In this kind of IPO, really a type of crowdfunding utilizing cybercurrency, tokens are purchased in the digital world by investors and traded in exchange for legal tender or other cybercurrencies such as Bitcoin. The methodology avoids many regulatory burdens and costs, and hence can be risky.

Private ICOs are becoming more common. For example,

serial entrepreneur Mike Marcus, an experienced veteran of startups with a personal background in information technology, sought to raise $50 million to fund an Artificial Intelligence-based company, Pensor. Pensor's mission is to collect and organize career, healthcare or legal documents that often go astray as Millenials enter the job market and Baby Boomers work on their retirement planning. With 40 million caregivers in the United States alone, the need is immense, as documents ranging from lists of medications to home inventories for property insurance purposes to trusts and wills must be at hand in case of emergency. One of the most compelling arguments made by Pensor is that subscribers need not learn any new coding or software languages, and because they encrypt all their documents personally using Pensor software, the company never sees their information. Back-up copies are kept in the Cloud in case the subscriber loses his mobile devices. As the company enters new industry verticals such as education, the template is copied throughout. Subscribers have control of their information in a secure fashion, and companies such insurers and banks like the system because compliance with their requirements is assured.

The creativity of the financial geniuses who continue to develop new market exchanges and new financial products truly is unrivaled. The results can be wonderful for investors and entrepreneurs alike. It is paramount, though, for all concerned to be transparent and to understand the implications of their commitment.

Remember, the financial community is full of agendas. I was very excited one morning to check my smartphone and see an alert from the *Seeking Alpha* website that one of the companies I follow had reported earnings and had a "beat." The much-sought-after "beat" means a company exceeded expectations in earnings or revenue, or both. Now, *Seeking Alpha* publishes notices and reports from free-lancers or independents rather than paid staff. Imagine my disappointment when I read the entire press release from the company and learned that the company had actually reported a steep loss on minimal revenue, which indicated its current share price of $1.82, compared to $3 the previous year, was justified. Somebody pushing this positive story had a very elastic definition of a "beat!"

The existence of shares that are publicly traded can sometimes lead even established companies to unusual places. In mid-2019 the board of Rite Aid voted to shrink its share count by 95% in a bid to push the remaining shares above the $1 minimum trading requirement of the New York Stock Exchange. The board of the troubled drugstore chain approved a 1-for-20 ratio for a reserve stock split after shareholders approved the plan. That cut the total number of outstanding shares from nearly 1.1 billion to about 54 million! The shares were trading at 57 cents before the split-adjusted basis. With the dramatic shrinkage in the number of shares, Rite Aid was able to maintain its status as a public company.

It is a definite best practice to have the right team in place if you are looking at a major funding event. Specifically, having an investor relations program in place prior to an IPO is critical to managing the pivotal transition to the rigors of the public markets during the months prior to the IPO, immediately following the initial public offering and through the duration of being a public company. Well in advance of the IPO, it is important to gather advisers who can assist the management team in creating such a program. Most importantly, the IR program can help raise the financial community's awareness of the company and educate analysts about its potential. A properly run investor relations program, according to third-party industry research, can mean as much as a double-digit increase in the stock price.

THE LONG RUNWAY TO GOING PUBLIC

Investor relations, legal and website advisers should prepare the board of directors and the management team for life as a public company by developing the organizational infrastructure and the comprehensive IR plan required to ensure compliance with SEC and exchange regulations, to create a consistent flow of corporate news and executive visibility, and to generate new investors and sell-side analyst coverage. These activities are designed to provide a sophisticated presence among Wall Street professionals, which will help the newly public company achieve its long-term objectives. Some key steps:

- Form a disclosure committee and draft disclosure procedures and a communications policy to guide the process of releasing news to the public, including spokesperson responsibilities and policies involving use of social media. The SEC's Reg FD (Full Disclosure) and applicable case law, as well as the disclosure policies of the exchanges, are critical touchstone documents.
- Establish corporate governance to ensure full compliance with SEC requirements such as SOX, Reg FD, Regulation G, and others. Prepare in advance for issues such as say-on-pay and director independence. Today, these are often critical issues for shareholders, the media, or even activists searching for corporate vulnerabilities, as public

companies' proxy statements have increasingly become of interest to investors.

- Establish a peer group for benchmarking, valuation, and for purposes of marketing to the investment community.
- Research potential issues likely to influence investors as they consider investing in the IPO. Provide peer group earnings intelligence, including reviewing earnings reports. Transcripts and analyst research reports of the company's peer group will provide valuable insight into popular industry metrics and potential market hot buttons. Utilizing this intelligence, the IR consultants can help management build the investment case and messaging platform based upon sustainable fundamentals that will be marketed to potential investors and analysts before the IPO and will provide ongoing momentum for the company and its stock after the IPO.
- IR Counsel will need to assess media coverage based upon LexisNexis database, or a similar comprehensive database to develop a benchmark for potential media coverage down the road.
- Draft an IR activities plan with a calendar for the next year, including quiet periods, earnings release dates, quarterly conference calls, SEC filing deadlines, potential investor conferences, and potential non-deal roadshow dates.
- Create investor materials to keep current and potential shareholders and analysts up to date, as well as to introduce the story to others who did not participate in the offering. These materials would

include the roadshow presentation (updated after each quarterly conference call), the IR Web site and investor kits for in-person meetings.

- Build an IR infrastructure to effectively drive activities after the quiet period is over, including developing relationships with potential stakeholders and analysts. Determine which Wall Street analysts could potentially cover the company on the sell-side or purchase the stock on the buy-side by garnering insights about the peer group buy-side and sell-side investment communities. These targets will become the foundation from which to conduct outreach post-IPO.

- Establish protocols, policies and procedures for quarterly reporting, which is the heart of a public company's ongoing communications with Wall Street.

  – Develop a process for quarterly earnings announcements.

  – Draft a quarterly earnings release template to capture the most important messages and to communicate the meaning of the company's financial results and performance in a clear, concise manner.

  – Draft a conference call template which offers company executives an opportunity to put a face on the company, build relationships, eliminate misperceptions, and position their company as an industry leader.

  – Select one or more vendors for release distribution, conference call, and webcast hosting.

– Plan to schedule follow-up calls with large stakeholders and sell-side analysts after each quarterly conference call.

- Draft a quarterly board report template to keep the board apprised of valuation and growth metrics, shareholder base information, and IR activities.
- Develop the investor relations website, a major project.
- Develop a plan for post-IPO IR activities, including:
- Conduct a shareholder identification and analysis to determine the composition of the current shareholder base.
- Generate new qualified institutional buy-side and sell-side targets.
- Implement an investor and media outreach strategy.
- Conduct a perception study to gauge the company's performance (six months to one year after IPO).
- Host an investor day (one year after IPO).

Momentum for a company and its stock post-IPO is typically developed pre-IPO in the planning stages. And with these checklists in hand, clear and transparent communication between the public company and the investment community will be all but assured.

THE IPO "BEST PRACTICES" CHECKLIST

- Select partners to comprise the IPO team— investment banks, law firm, accounting firm, investor relations firm, website vendor.

- Form a disclosure committee and draft disclosure procedures and a communications policy.
- Establish corporate governance procedures.
- Conduct training session on corporate governance, Reg FD, and how to communicate as a public company.
- Provide spokesperson training and presentation training as required.
- Establish a peer group for benchmarking.
- Research potential issues likely to influence investors as they consider investing in the IPO.
- Build the investment case and messaging platform.
- Assess media coverage.
- Draft an IR activities plan.
- Create investor materials.
- Build an IR infrastructure to market to Wall Street post-IPO.
- Establish protocols, policies, and procedures for quarterly reporting.
- Draft a quarterly board report template.
- Develop the investor relations website.
- Secure "day-of" media coverage.
- Introduce management to top investment bankers and analysts.
- Develop a plan for post-IPO IR activities.

THE IR WEBSITE

The IR portion of the company website is all-important, as it draws both institutional and individual investors and houses major company documents such as earnings releases and investor presentations in one easy-to-find place. Though the purpose and goals of a website will vary based on the needs of each company, it is critical. Consider that the average American spends 7.5 hours a day with some form of digital media. For many, the IR site serves as the archive of record for all historical public disclosure, while others view it as the primary method of disclosure itself. For some, the site is simply used to maintain compliance with SEC regulations. In the optimal case, it not only acts a regulatory channel but also as an opportunity for a company to outline its unique story to the investment community. Regardless of the perspective, a great website serves as an easy way to communicate important information to a large number of investors or analysts in real time, in a consistent manner.

Amid all of the IPO preparation going on in-house, however, this valuable communications tool for investors (especially for potential investors) is often overlooked. Getting the investor relations website up and running is a critical element of the IPO process, as newly public companies will see high traffic leading up to, and on the first day of trading. As with so much of the IPO process, review by outside counsel is essential. Some of the discussion with outside counsel can be quite frustrating, some can be quite illuminating, but it is essential. In one case, the legal team put significant restrictions on what the company could put on the website for fear of pre-marketing the securities to anyone outside the roadshow attendees until 30 days after the IPO was priced. Another set of arguments ensued when counsel objected to identifying the management team because it might give confidence to non-roadshow investors that the company would be well-managed! From a strictly legal perspective looking at the website, while there are only a few must-haves, there are a whole range of opportunities to go beyond simply meeting regulatory requirements.

Let's take a look at some of the most important areas for consideration:

- Regulatory background
- Considerations for building out the website
- Readying the website for IPO Day

Surprisingly, there are actually very few iron-clad IR website requirements from the perspective of the SEC, with most recommended content coming from the major exchanges, the New York Stock Exchange and the NASDAQ or federal law. First and foremost, under the Sarbanes-Oxley Act, all public companies that maintain corporate websites are required to post on those sites their Section 16 filings outlining activity by beneficial owners by the end of the business day after the report is filed with the SEC. Each report must remain posted for at least 12 months. This, in and of itself, does not seem very significant. However, it represents the base of what the IR website has come to embody—open and transparent communication. By making these filings easily accessible to the public on its corporate website, the company is actively inviting investors to review the activity of the company's largest and most influential shareholders. Rather than forcing investors to third parties, the company's website now becomes the source.

In 2005, starting with their voluntary filer program, the SEC initiated the ruling that requires that all filing public companies must provide their financial statements on their corporate websites in interactive data format using the eXtensible Business Reporting Language (XBRL). This applies specifically to a company's 10-K and 10-Q filings. When initiating this requirement, the SEC noted that the new rules were intended to make financial information easier for investors to analyze, further driving the importance of clear and transparent communication between public companies and investors.

Effective in 2009, the SEC enacted the "Notice & Access" amendments to proxy rules, which outlined how public companies were required to make proxy materials available to investors, including via their corporate website. These materials must be in a format that allows reading, searching and printing (PDF is acceptable), and the materials must be posted such that they protect the anonymity of a person accessing that website, meaning that site cannot use tracking cookies that reveal an individual's identity and behavior. This naturally fits very nicely within the theme of improving the way public companies communicate with their investors, and the ease with which investors can access important information via the company's corporate website.

While these are all relatively straightforward requirements, they do require a fine-tuned process to execute efficiently, and to ensure ongoing compliance. This is where the decision comes to choose between using a third party for IR website hosting or rely on an existing web team to host the investor relations section in-house.

One of the biggest advantages of using a third party is that most of the work is already taken care of. These solutions should be fully equipped to handle all aspects of regulatory compliance, as well as to provide additional tools and content to make investors' and analysts' lives easier. These could include advanced charting functionality, and deeper content like ownership data, M&A activity, credit ratings, and capital structure information that would be tedious to maintain internally. By providing additional data and functionality above and beyond what's required, it helps to make the IR website a trusted destination for company information, and ultimately helps to draw traffic that might otherwise go to Yahoo Finance or similar sources.

It should be noted that, while the majority of public companies use a third-party vendor for web hosting, both approaches (in-house and third-party solutions) are perfectly viable options. Companies of all industries and sizes have employed each approach successfully. The main criteria for making that decision should be based on whether the solution is:

- Easy to implement and manage
- Easy for investors to use on a regular basis
- Flexible enough to evolve and grow with the newly public company

Building out the IR website from scratch is no small undertaking and the process should begin well ahead of the IPO date. When working with pre-IPO companies, I generally suggest a minimum of 4-6 weeks to get the site built, reviewed, edited, and 100% ready for launch. Companies need not only to consider how regulatory compliance will be maintained, but also how they want to reflect and communicate their investment strategy. The website should really reflect how the company presents itself to investors in any context (roadshow, investor conference, quarterly results call), so the IPO roadshow presentation is a great place to start. Managers should ask themselves:

- What do we want investors to know about our strategy?
- What materials and mediums will we use to communicate this? (presentations, financial supplements, video)

- How, and in what formats do investors prefer to receive this information? (PDF/Excel documents, email alerts, press releases, social media)

A good start is to look at what industry peers are doing, but the best and most valuable feedback will come from investors and analysts themselves. If using an IR consultant and/or a website vendor, they should be able to provide guidance and help you understand the practice that make the most sense for your company.

Lastly, when building out the website for the IPO, two things cannot be understated:

First, consistency is critical. When building out a section or page, always make sure you won't run into impediments down the road when updates or changes need to be made. For example, if quarterly earnings materials are posted in certain formats in certain areas on the website, producing, adding, and updating those materials on a quarterly basis should be straightforward so the process can be done quickly, efficiently, and without error. If there is potential for last-minute changes to an earnings presentation, it shouldn't post in a section of the website that takes 48 hours to update.

Second, the team responsible for hosting the IR website should be a partner that can proactively make suggestions, provide best practices guidance, and understand the role your IR site plays in your investor relations program. The IPO process is a great opportunity to leverage their knowledge and experience, as well as to solidify and practice those procedures that will reoccur on a weekly, monthly, quarterly, or annual basis. For example, we recommend staging a mock earnings day to understand timing and uncover any risks or trouble areas. This makes the IPO process more comfortable, as well as building an ongoing trust and comfort level when high priority scenarios arise such as merger announcements or surprise industry developments.

There is a lot to consider when thinking about your overall web strategy, but the good news is that you don't need to start out with everything at once. Almost every IPO client we've worked with in the past has strategically added new content as it becomes relevant and they mature as a public company. For instance, the first earnings cycle might mark the initiation of a dividend, and at that point they would want to add a page that outlines their dividend payment policy and history. For that reason, we've compiled a checklist of critical items for the IPO launch day:

General website requirements:

- Clear and visible link from the corporate website home page
- One-click access
- Easy to remember URL
- Design/Branding continuity with the corporate website
- Reliable 24/7 accessibility
- Tried and tested web host with redundancy plans
- Ability to measure traffic and browsing trends
- Environment free from tracking cookies that can identify individual users
- Mobile compatibility
- Automatic redirect to mobile version of website
- Consistency of content on desktop/mobile—utilize same source to eliminate need for multiple updates

Content/Usability:

- Company overview and mission statement—why invest in your company?
- SEC filings—Automated
- Section 16 filings
- Accessible formats (PDF, HTML, Excel)
- Minimum 1-year archive (full historical record is recommended)
- XBRL filings—Automated, preferably with a built-in reader
- Press releases—Automated
- Corporate governance information
- Officers and Directors
- Governance Documents—Code of Ethics, Insider Trading Policy, etc.
- Committee Composition
- Committee Charters
- Detailed contact information
- Pricing information—Automated
- Live and historical pricing feeds
- Charting
- Investor presentations
- Automated email alerts for important content sets
- Social feeds and links (if being utilized for investor relations)
- RSS feeds for important content sets
- Full text/document search

Getting the IR website ready for IPO day isn't a small or unimportant task by any means, but it doesn't have to be an arduous one. With preparation, a good head start, and employing the right team of people to advise and support you through the process, getting the IR website launched on or ahead of IPO will be a smooth experience. As the U.S. Marine Corps likes to say, "Slow is smooth, and smooth is fast."

BENEFITS AND BURDENS

As should be obvious by now, going public isn't for everybody. Careful thought and planning is needed before undertaking to meet the rigors of the public markets. In particular, the staffing, time, and planning needed to build an investor audience is immense. Writing, editing, and rehearsing multiple drafts of scripts for quarterly earnings calls—for larger companies, a dozen or more drafts would not be unusual—is time consuming and sometimes irritating. Press releases, filings, and often follow-up calls with institutional investors even after the quarterly call is done occupy a huge percentage of management's attention.

And then there are the roadshows, meeting with institutions at their place of business, or restaurants or hotels, around the country, for periodic updates. Also, any investment bank worth its salt stages its own investor conferences at times and places of its choosing, usually in five-star hotels or resorts at major cities. Company officials arrive in person, well-rehearsed, to give stand-up presentations to large groups of current and prospective investors, and to do more personal one-on-one meetings. At these one-on-ones, many firms who take pride in their own analysis and intelligence try to ask questions that will enable them to develop financial models superior to their peers. They also, of course, want to develop a rapport with management and gauge their quality.

One such conference that is one of the biggest draws is the

annual conference held by Newport Beach-based Roth Capital every March at a seaside resort in Dana Point, California. The spring timing and Southern California location are a big draw to Midwesterners and East Coasters worn out by several months of nasty weather. But the true draw is a sizable group—in the hundreds, believe it or not—of public and private companies that present and meet with the financial community. Vendors of every stripe also attend, offering their services as corporate enablers with everything from websites to accounting to public relations to legal representation. Surprisingly, the dress code is not California casual, but business suits. The conference has a dark-suited seriousness belied by the sight of bankers and executives cradling their iPhones on Adirondack chairs at the Ritz-Carlton atop a cliff overlooking the Pacific Ocean with surfers in sight on the waves below.

The event's host, Roth Capital, a West Coast firm founded by legendary investors Byron and Eli Roth, has an influence that extends far beyond its size, which for most firms would lead to being classified as a regional rather than national outfit. It caters to somewhat younger, smaller, faster-growing companies than the norm, in categories such as pharma, biotech, cleantech, technology and media, and so forth. At its flagship three-day conference in southern California, printed agendas are a thing of the past; these hip attendees use a smart configured app to track their appointments. The conference itself, now in its 35th year, is unusual in that it features many privately held companies that may consider going public or are seeking funds while private. It brings together more than 500 public and private companies and approximately 1,000 investors to provide attendees with investment ideas. The event is also well attended by the family offices, the business offices of wealthy families, who are scouting investments and networking with other family offices or investment banks. All in all, it is an American celebration of entrepreneurship and creativity worthy of the Medicis.

Some conferences focus on industry sectors, such as energy, biotech, cleantech, mining, or media. The annual Allen conference in Sun Valley, Idaho, held by the investment bank founded by Herb Allen, combines family fun with presentations in the world of media and tech, and has become famous for the deals spawned by the industry moguls in attendance. There are also numerous industry trade shows attended by bankers looking for clients and representing clients. In some cases bankers will sponsor a day or two of investment conferences before or after the tradeshow, a highly efficient means for Corporate America to generate product revenue at one venue, then seek deals and financing at other.

In addition, some firms that conduct only pure research to sell, without doing transactions or other deals that generate fees, also hold their own conferences. The Sidoti conferences in New York, catering to smaller companies in different industries and life cycles, require an entrance fee but are well worth the cost as they attract several hundred potential investors at each event. The Nobel Financial winter conference, held at an attractive venue in Florida during the season when Midwesterners and East Coasters are eager to hear company pitches in good weather, is another good example. In the Midwest, Barrington Research holds a Chicago conference that does not include company presentations but emphasizes one-on-one, personal meetings between investor and company. All are worth of consideration depending upon budget and management time and inclination.

For companies seeking investment banks offering transaction advice as well as research, there are many to choose from, often in the form of a "bank beauty contest" or "bank bake-off" competitive review. In their efforts to get to the head of the pack, many banks will seek to build a relationship long before the IPO is contemplated by meeting with management as headquarters, viewing their products at trade shows, or visiting company manufacturing facilities. Plenty of banks are interested in smaller companies and can offer industry expertise and contacts for purposes of revenue growth, financing or merger and acquisition advice.

However, as always, let the buyer beware. It's important for the company to have a realistic understanding of what a bank can and cannot do. Likewise, bank fees must be carefully weighed, with the corporation considering its preference in paying a monthly fee (almost always debited against the success fee at the completion of the transaction), as well as the success fees for generating a certain goal of financing or completing an acquisition deal. Warren Buffett famously described investment bankers as "fee-charging middlemen."

Mr. Buffett's description correctly suggests that the riches of an IPO and being public do not extend to everyone, despite the popular imagination. Many employees who are compensated heavily with stock in the early days of a company instead of cash have rose-colored glasses about the payback. In some cases, so do the owners and founders! Explaining in a companywide memo why SpaceX was not pursuing an IPO, founder Elon Musk told the workforce, "Public company stocks, particularly if big-step changes in technology are involved, go through extreme volatility, both for reasons of internal execution and for reasons that have nothing to do with anything, except the economy ... For those who are under the impression they are so clever that they can outsmart public market investors and would sell SpaceX stock at the 'right time,' let me relieve you of any such notion ... Selling public company stock with insider knowledge is illegal. As a result, selling public company stock is restricted to narrow time windows a few times a year."

With this douse of cold water on expectations of future riches, Elon was doing his employees a favor. Elon seems to have a good understanding of what venture capitalists, investment bankers, and other moneymen actually do.

Venture capitalists, for starters, have a true expertise in understanding how much money it actually takes to run a certain kind and size of company. Investment bankers—the people Warren Buffett famously disparaged as "fee-charging middlemen"—use their analysts and software programs to run models predicting the future returns of investments in a wide variety of categories. One young biotech company I worked with was successful in its application to the Food & Drug Administration to approve the only oral drug in the U.S. to diagnose adult growth hormone deficiency. Since the number of people afflicted with this disease was well-known and it was possible to estimate the percentage of the market this product could obtain, as it was both cheaper and faster than previously methods of diagnosis, smart analysts could easily predict the revenue and possible profits of the company. The good news is, the company and its investors could rely on a predictable model from credible sources; the bad news, there was limited upside unless the company could successfully buy or create other "orphan" drugs.

Long and short of it, don't even think about undertaking financing without a trusted advisor. With the right team in place, you'll avoid bear territory and enjoy the coveted realms of the bull and the unicorn.

8

CASHING IN ON CANNABIS

The previous chapter's discussion of mainstream branding would be incomplete without a tour of the fastest-growing industry in the world, cannabis. What happens when an illegal industry suddenly becomes not only legal but highly regulated?

How do companies in this crowded field of growers, dispensaries and producers of niche products distinguish themselves from others?

The cannabis industry is booming, both in retail sales and in the stock market. With its penchant for bad puns, *Bloomberg Business Week* called the business the "pot of gold." Momentum built quickly after October 17, 2018, when Canada legalized usage completely. Certainly, the early investors, entrepreneurs and investors benefited greatly.

In the U.S., legalization has been more piecemeal. Some states such as Colorado took leading positions, while more conservative venues such as Michigan, Illinois, or North Dakota authorized medical marijuana while deciding later if the drug should be legal for adults 21 and older. Many companies entered the market initially by introducing products infused with cannabidiol (CBD), a chemical found in cannabis and hemp plants believed to treat many medical conditions without providing the mind-altering "high" connected with another cannabis-related chemical, tetrahydrocannabinol (THC). The giant retail pharmacy CVS had CBD-infused products on its shelves in only eight states in 2019. By 2023, 22 states had legalized cannabis to some degree.

The trouble is, the federal government still considers marijuana a "Schedule 1" drug (regulated akin to heroin), which has made commercial banks reluctant to loan money and investment banks reluctant to broker deals.

Moreover, legalization of use does not require legalization of availability. Many large cities restrict the sale of cannabis products to specified districts, and many town councils have voted down allowing such products to be sold at retail in their towns.

With more tolerant laws and policies in Canada, companies such as Canopy Growth, one of the largest producers by market capitalization, and the small Canadian investment banks that supported the industry did well in the early initial public offerings.

Publicly traded U.S. cannabis companies raised more than $2 billion in capital, typically listing on the Canadian exchanges given the more easy-going environment north of the border.

To compete, the U.S. side has seen a push at the state level to change banking laws so that the cannabis world has a currency other than cash. Not surprisingly, the leading law firm for cannabis companies, the Hoban Law Group, is based in Colorado, the pacesetter in medical and recreational cannabis legalization.

Still to be widely publicized, of course, are the inevitable stock scams and fraudulent operations that come with any attractive market. These may be in the form of "pump and dump" schemes in which founders "pump" the price of the stock through mailings and overly optimistic or outright fraudulent claims. They then "dump" the stock at its high, crashing the stock price, taking their huge returns and leaving investors with big losses. The typical pump-and-dump solicitation is a robocall or email along the lines of, "Invest fifty dollars and retire a millionaire." Sound too good to be true? It usually is.

Even in the legal field of e-cigarette smokers, major brands can be vulnerable to product quality and regulatory issues. Altria wrote down its investment in Juul Labs, the best-known maker of flavored e-cigarettes, by $4.5 billion, due to increased regulatory pressure and investigation into alleged product contamination.

The lesson is, every fast-growing industry category are subject to fast-changing winds of political sentiment, product safety and quality issues, regulatory scrutiny, and fickle consumer tastes.

For now, for the real cannabis players, business is smoking.

The numbers are truly amazing. In the U.S. alone, about 18% of adults claim to be current pot users. The legal market in 2022 was estimated to be worth about $16.7 billion, but the illegal market is estimated to actually be about 75% of the total market.

Moreover, legalization is a tailwind. According to the Colorado Department of Public Health & Environment, at the time of legalization in 2014, about 13.6% of adults used marijuana at least once a month; by 2017, the number was 15.5%.

However, growing pot even in controlled conditions can be as dodgy as growing any row crop in the Midwest. The plant's CBD and THC potencies can vary greatly. Standardizing production of the numerous hemps, oils, isolates, distillates, and concentrates extracted from the plant is an industry-wide challenge. Branding and retailing for consumer and medicinal uses is no easier than with any other retail or pharma product. Weed companies can't get federal trademarks for some parts of their business, so protecting the offbeat names, similar to those used by craft beers, used at the dispensaries will be difficult. Brands such as Kiwi Sunk, SharksBreath, Alien Bubba, Granola Funk may never be household names, but they may well find a broader audience.

On the plus side, the creativity of producers beyond the obvious products is breathtaking. The founder of Jelly Bellies, a company that he had sold, began producing CBD-infused Jelly Bellies under a different name. Vitalibis, a small, OTC-traded formulator of hemp-based wellness products containing naturally occurring CBD (cannabidiol), emphasizing safety and quality.

To meet the unique business services needs of the industry, smaller law firms and accounting firms around the country began affiliating with the established firms, such as Hoban. Complying with industry-specific taxes, handling income tax returns or trying to secure hard-to-find banking services, navigating uncharted waters of employee and employer rights, is all part of the tangle. Even services such as property insurance and liability insurance are needed, as the industry involves dispensaries, storage facilities, distributors, processors, manufacturers, and private cannabis testing facilities and laboratories.

No wonder that, as of 2019, everybody wanted in. Casinos want to buy or invest in cannabis-related companies. Big Tobacco in the form of Altria, famous for its Marlboro brand of cigarettes, has taken nearly a $2 billion stake in a grower, Cronos. Constellation Brands, owner of Corona beer, placed a huge $4 billion bet on the cannabis industry by investing in Canopy. The mom and pop investors, the so-called "retail" market (non-institutional investors, in other words) have had a feeding frenzy.

I knew the momentum for the industry was well underway when an investor relations exec I know turned down a lucrative job at an established retailer for an IPO'ing cannabis company. Pax Labs, a maker of cannabis vaping equipment, completed a $445 million financing in two rounds in mid-2019. Top-notch hedge funds such as Chase Colman's Tiger Growth Funds participated in the financing, establishing Pax as a unicorn with a valuation of $1 billion.

Likewise, aside from the big companies making direct investments, the M&A game is now big money. In early 2019, Harvest Health & Recreation paid $850 million for cannabis operator Verano Holdings, creating the nation's largest legal distributor of marijuana.

Another big player, Aurora, actually retained an activist investor, Nelson Pelz, who is well known for investing in companies or buying them and adding marketing expertise, as an advisor. The company's stock immediately shot up upon the news.

Even the CBD market is hot. One producer, CBD Lion LLC, was acquired by Acquired Sales Corp., a PE firm, for $2 million in cash and stock. CBD Lion sales had grown from $4,000 a month to $160,000 a month, all in products such as CBD-infused vapes, gummies, lotions and the like.

In a nutshell, I think portfolio shaping will be where the big money is for this industry. With financial savvy, even a small firm could acquire larger competitors or find worthwhile companies in adjacent markets. Fitting the pieces together in a profitable, high-growth shape is the management challenge, but there are plenty of people who can do this.

Yet marketing products can be a grey area, as the biggest cannabis retailer, Curaleaf Holdings, was warned by the Food &

Drug Administration that its lotion, pain-relief patch, tincture, and disposable vape pen are considered to be drugs because they purport to treat pain, anxiety, and other conditions. While legal, CBD has not been approved by the FDA for use as an ingredient in food and beverages. Even pet products, a huge market, will need to be regulated, as the FDA monitors therapeutic claims.

And ironically, major states that have legalized cannabis such as California and New York, both desperate for the tax dollars generated by the industry, have found the biggest threat to be the growers and shops not registered with the state. These illegals can sell their product at steep discounts to the legal registered shops which deal with taxation rates up to 40%. The rationale for charging a premium, such as safety and regulated sales, pales in comparison to the cheaper prices offered by unregistered sellers. In 2022 California had illegal sales of $8.1 billion compared to legal sales of $5.4 billion, according to New Frontier Data, an analytics firm. And often the penalties when the regulatory laws are enforced amount to a ticket, so the illegal shops barely take a beat before continuing their sales. New York City today has five licensed shops as opposed to an estimated 1,400 bodegas and shops that are selling without a license.

Here's the cannabis conundrum. Conventional wisdom would argue the easy play in this sector would be to bet on companies in the supply chain that you like as acquisition targets. The easy play, maybe, but not necessarily the smart play. In cannabis I take a contrarian view and would argue the highest returns will come from identifying the acquirers, not the acquisition targets. As acquisition-minded players do their deals, they will achieve economies of scale and will drive rapid growth through internal organic means and acquisition. Look for companies dedicated to transparency and compliance, such as Chicago-based Cresco Labs (OTCMKTS: CRLBF) and others. That solves the cannabis conundrum of how to participate in this new industry, with its legal status in turmoil at local, state, and federal levels and a plethora of brands rising and falling, while minimizing your risks.

9

BE A MASTER OF DISASTER

It was a hot, sunny, muggy May morning in 1996 when the doors to Miami-to-Atlanta ValuJet® flight 592 were sealed. Several of the airline workers had family members on board and thought nothing of it, as it's common for airline workers to live in one city and work in another, commuting by air much the way most of us commute by car, bus or train.

Yet only minutes later, the flight slammed into the Everglades swamp after an onboard fire, with 109 souls aboard.

The public relations chief and the CEO at the time were at a business breakfast in Atlanta when they got the call on their cell phones. Colleagues told the female PR exec later that, when she heard the voice on the other end of the line recap the news, her face turned absolutely white.

The pair rushed back to headquarters to prepare for the onslaught of media calls, family grief and regulatory scrutiny that was to ensue. What occurred was years of legal entanglement, accusations of disregard of safety, a lurch to near-bankruptcy for the airline, and the near-end of the business category it had helped to create: low-fare leisure travel.

The six-page Sunday feature that the *Atlanta Journal* ran on the crash with the headline "We Know There's No Hope" was only the beginning.

Moreover, the fallout from this horrific accident in the Everglades would have been magnified even more if social media had been available. This is the kind of story that would have gone viral in minutes. Imagine the texts and calls that would have been sent from the smartphones of the doomed passengers had that technology existed.

ValuJet had been a Southern success story and a stock-market highflier. An entrepreneurial miracle, the airline had been highly praised for making airline travel affordable for the masses. Other airlines joined in, following its example, including the company that became the industry leader, Herb Kelleher's Dallas-based Southwest Airlines.

It all came to a tragic end when the Federal Aviation Administration questioned ValuJet's safety practices, and the low-fare air sector's as well. The fire had been caused, it was learned, when an oxygen canister stowed in the plane's cargo hold had been improperly secured. These are the canisters that feed the yellow oxygen masks that drop down from above in event of a cabin pressure emergency. Years later it was determined the canister supplier had been at fault, but for those precious years, ValuJet took the blame. The airline's relationships with the leisure and business traveler, the FAA and other government authorities, individual and institutional investors, and the local communities it served, were irretrievably broken.

Experts in crisis communications know that in situations involving death, company response must be on a quite different scale from a "slip and fall" case, a product recall, or financial malfeasance. This is true whether the company has some culpability or is simply an innocent victim of, say, a burglary gone wrong.

The lesson for business owners is: Effective crisis response is a competitive advantage.

Clearly, passengers needed to trust in the airline's safety, and investors needed to trust in its ability to generate revenue and profits again. By 1998 the airline that had been the darling of Wall Street and the flying public had nearly gone bust.

Research showed that the flying public would never trust ValuJet. Nearly 25% of former passengers said the airline was "unsafe" and nearly 50% said they were "very unlikely" to fly it again. This was the death knell for the ValuJet brand, the board of directors recognized.

A search was commenced for a new name. The one that emerged from a long copyright search, AirTran®, was generally not viewed as perfect. Some people said it sounded like an airline limo service. That said, the number of available brand names for a regional airline was quite limited. AirTran, while not perfect, would have to do.

But the rebranding had to be more than cosmetic. New management came in with a story to tell. The plan was to transform the airline into more of a service for business fliers, who typically are used to expensing their travel and paying higher fares, as they often have to fly on short notice. Management was able to negotiate with Boeing to become the launch airline for a new Boeing regional jet, the 717, which would be configured with more side-by-side seating rather than the cramped three-seats-per-row that most low-fare fliers were accustomed to. A radical new rewards program enabled frequent fliers to quickly earn free flights. As the expectations of business travelers are different from those of leisure travelers, the staff at the gates and onboard needed new training to deal with these passengers.

The new strategy and the new planes were unveiled at a press conference at the Atlanta airport to a crowd of print, TV and radio journalists, and employees excited about the change. Tours of one of the new airplanes were permitted, with plenty of photo and video coverage. Company officials and government officials gave speeches outlining the importance of reliable air service to local communities and the operational changes that had been made to ensure safety and comfort onboard.

In a bit of showmanship, when the guests walked down to the end of the concourse for the event, all the signage at the gates still said ValuJet, with the old logo and name. By the time they left, staff had switched out all the posters, billboards, and other signage to the new logo and branding. The large *A* against a green background, a professional scheme of colors also matched the exterior of the gleaming new Boeing planes with their Rolls Royce® engines. The annual report for that first year picked up this theme, with a giant cover shot of a worker polishing the *A* on the tail of a brand-new plane. Inside the book, dramatic color photos of employees, ranging from a female flight captain to ramp agents and customer service agents, presented the smiling faces that would greet incoming passengers.

We ran ads to explain openly that ValuJet would henceforth be known as AirTran rather than trying to hide the fact. Brand messages associating the airline with Boeing and Rolls-Royce, both well-known and respected brands, reinforced the high safety standards of AirTran in the minds of fliers.

Credibility was immediately restored. Overnight, the company's share price rebounded by 30%, adding $50 million to the company's stock market capitalization. Fares were up double digits within two weeks. Breakeven was reached quickly. But to survive and prosper long-term, the airline had to achieve an average fare of $65 and a load factor (percentage of seats filled) of 60%.

Management stuck to its game plan, and by opening new markets, advertising, public relations programs that reached both travelers and the financial community, the company continued to grow. Several of the airline workers who had said goodbye to their family members on the fatal flight continued to work for the company, a testament to the quality of its culture. By mid-2000, the load factor had reached 70.4%, 10 points higher than the baseline goal, and the average ticket price was $80, $15 higher than the $65 goal.

This success did not go unnoticed. By 2011, AirTran was acquired by Southwest Airlines® for a premium price, bringing the entire journey from the nightmarish crash to the business revival, full circle.

PLANNING FOR DISASTER

The AirTran case would have been considerably different in today's world as it took place in its entirety without the universal usage of smartphones, email, social media, and other tools that are now pervasive. News of the disaster itself would have spread in a viral fashion, but also, company communicators would have had more tools at their command to dispel rumors and share accurate information. Social media today has to be a major factor in company planning.

A somewhat similar fact pattern occurred in 2023 with the implosion of the small Titan sub in which five people perished at the bottom of the ocean. Lack of public response from the sub operator OceanGate along with piecemeal revelations of prior safety concerns quickly led to calls for the extreme vacationing business segment to be regulated.

The keys to weathering a crisis are preventive thinking, contingency planning, communicating quickly and honestly, and taking remedial measures as appropriate.

The company that takes these steps to manage a crisis is likely not only to survive, but to prosper.

Misleading ads, product recalls, improper executive compensation—in rueful hindsight, these are the kinds of crises that could have been averted. Programs that comply with legal and regulatory standards pay for themselves.

In contrast, acts of evil—workplace shootings, arson, sabotage—can never be foreseen, but they *can* be prepared for.

If your company has a code of conduct, a mission statement, or a statement of values, each of your programs should be measured against this code. In addition, test your programs against statements of ethics from the American Marketing Association, the Public Relations Society of America, and your trade and professional groups.

If your company lacks such a statement, you should urge senior management and your board to develop one. An easy way to begin is by retaining a consultant to review your business and marketing practices. This review might uncover areas that can be challenged by activists, the media and regulators.

Using this research as a planning aid, a crisis contingency plan should be prepared by the legal, marketing, operations and PR teams. That plan must include:

- Major areas of vulnerability (risk)
- Approved company spokespeople, with home, mobile and office phone numbers and emails
- Outside resources, such as public relations firms, law firms, compliance or ethics consultants, trade associations, and government or regulatory officials,

with phone numbers and emails addresses if
possible
- Lists of business, consumer, and trade media
- A general action plan of how the company will
respond to anticipated events

In recent decades, ethical and regulatory standards have become so critical that companies have retained compliance officers, most of whom are lawyers, and consultants, to advise them. These in-house experts and consultants who manage internal investigations, whistleblower hotlines, and other situations are confidential counselors. They should play a role in developing and implementing the crisis plan.

After all, not even the best compliance efforts and contingency planning may be able to forestall a crisis. However, they are essential actions in helping a company organize a prepared response to the media and public, marshal its resources to fix the problem, and defend itself against unwarranted charges.

Using the contingency plan as a guide in the event of a crisis, one of the first steps is to determine what's really at stake for the company. You must work closely with senior management, PR counsel, and legal counsel to assess risks and responses.

You need to verify the facts of situation immediately. Only the facts can show the culpability, if any, of the company. Are you being singled out for a practice that is common for an entire industry? If so, your competitors just became your allies.

Ask these questions to assess the marketing risk to your company: Does the incident threaten the viability of a brand in which large dollars have been invested? What is the likelihood it will affect other brands? To what extent is the reputation of the corporate parent at risk? Is this a three-day news story or a recurring issue?

And I use the word "issue" advisedly. There can be a big difference between a crisis and an issue. The proper level of chemicals in ground water is an issue—but it can become a crisis immediately if there is a public health reaction based on that level, a report from a group disputing the proper level, or a fraudulent claim based on chemical contamination.

At the corporate financial level, for example, dealing with the so-called "shorts"—short investors who, unlike the typical long investor, are actually betting the stock will fall because of specific company or industry factors—is usually an ongoing issue. But management and boards sometimes elevate the issue to crisis levels when a short investor takes a position in the stock by their own surprised reactions. I've seen them publicly call a short investor "a liar"—an epithet that wasn't necessarily shared by others in the financial community who didn't participate in management's wounded pride. The short investor himself may draw attention to his bet in hopes of driving the stock price further downward. The West Coast short investor Andrew Left, for example, also publishes a newsletter that draws attention to his investment ideas. It's important for company management to not conflate an issue with a crisis if their company appears on a list of shorted stocks or their investment banker points out a rising percentage of short ownership.

That said, short interest in a stock is clearly a sign that something is wrong. Perhaps the market doesn't fully understand the company—or, even more sensitively, perhaps management doesn't under market. A perception study or a series of conversations with major shareholders would definitely be in order.

This gets to another key portion of the contingency plan, which is to enlist allies, third-party spokespeople, and other outside experts to support the company's position. Outside allies may include academics, interest groups, customers, think tanks, legislators, public officials, and trade associations. These external authorities all can provide additional, valuable credibility to a company whose ethical conduct is in question.

Post-crisis, or if there is a sales slump that may be caused by the harmful publicity, watch carefully to see if sales are returning. Determine the reactions of dealers and distributors, which can be done quickly through "soft soundings" carried out by salespeople. Monitor news coverage and conduct research to provide hard information about the gravity of the problem.

Here are some hard-won lessons from how from this abstract plan has actually been applied; the steps described below are ones I've taken successfully when I've handled crises such as closing a large manufacturing plant, a small family-owned chain of retail stores, and a casino. Note that with employment high and the economy performing well, one might think layoffs and facility closings would be fading memories of a recessionary past. Yet there are numerous incidents of both. The reason is the continuing wave of mergers, acquisitions and leveraged buyouts. Forced to slim down to pay off heavy debt loads, companies of all sizes must consolidate further. Offices and manufacturing plants will be shut or streamlined as facilities are rationalized or assets sold to other companies. Each closing incorporated into the case below was large enough to be covered under the Federal Worker Adjustment and Retraining Notification Act (WARN) as well as various state laws. Certainly, companies anticipating large layoffs (typically more than 50 people involved) and closings of facilities should consult three groups, maybe more, of internal or external resources. These are:

- Legal counsel experienced with WARN and labor law

- Public relations advisors skilled on communicating with media, the financial community, unions (if applicable), the local community, and other groups; and
- Human resources specialists

Clearly, the shutdown and layoff experience is traumatic for those even remotely connected with the process. The announcement is often nearly as stressful on those who must deliver the news as on those who receive it. And there is a "ripple effect" in the announcement that goes far beyond the affected site. A poorly handled closing and layoff can provoke severe reactions from local politicians, financial analysts, and customers. Management must reach the major constituencies of the company, ranging from investors to media to employees at the affected facility. Each constituency will react in a different way to the news.

This requires management to carefully think through the messages the company communicates to all its constituencies. It also required detailed execution of a plan to communicate the news, help affected employees adjust, and alleviate negative publicity. The need is to satisfy the legal, public relations, and human relations demands of the dislocation.

There are three major phases involved in planning the announcement.

PHASE ONE: PRELIMINARY PLANNING

Let's assume the decision has been made to phase out one or more facilities over a period of time. Logistical planning for the transfer of operations or ceasing to function as an ongoing business is underway. Or for whatever reason, a sizeable layoff is being planned. Making the announcement to employees and the outside world will soon be a reality. Let's think about the process.

The first step is to determine all the audiences or company constituencies the announcement must reach, and what the company must communicate to each group. What are their information needs? Management should compile a list of those groups who will be affected by the news. In addition to employees at the affected location, such a list might include media (business, trade, local, social media), shareholders, financial analysts, lenders, customers, suppliers, and employees throughout the company who may not be directly affected but will learn of the closing through the company grapevine. In fact, there is often a resident gossip whom I call "the head grape on the grapevine," and this is a person who ought to be briefed individually, probably informally, about what is going on, because he or she will be one of the first people others turn to for rumors and information. In pre-smartphone days, this grapevine would have taken place in the company cafeteria or the diner or bar after work; today it is equally as likely to be take place with a messaging app.

Next, for each major constituency, review the information needs of that group. Think of the one or two major messages that must be communicated. To employees at the affected location, it may well be: "We are launching an all-out effort to train you how to find another job, and we are telling employers in this area that our people will be looking for employment." To employees at locations unaffected by the layoffs, the message may be one of reassurance: "Location A is being closed to better serve our customers by transferring operations to Location B, which is closer to our major markets and more profitable. No further consolidations are planned."

Of course, the needs of a financial or industry analyst are considerably different from those of employees. The analyst is looking for information he needs to make an earnings forecast and adjust his computer model. The message to an analyst in general terms is: "We are downsizing the company and consolidating the plant to become more efficient and more profitable."

The facts are the same. The message to each constituency is different because the interests, concerns and information needs of that constituency are different.

When management has identified the key constituencies, and the key messages for each, the next step is to determine how to deliver the message to each group.

Then grid out the plan using Excel® or other management software as you prefer.

PHASE TWO: THE ANNOUNCEMENT

The ideal announcement strategy is simultaneous disclosure to all audiences. Employees shouldn't read about the closing in the morning's *Wall Street Journal*.

WARN requires 60 days advance notice in writing to employees. Giving notice includes providing notice to an employee's last known address or providing notice in paycheck envelopes and digital accounts. The law recognizes exceptions to compliance such as shutdowns due to nature disasters, labor disputes, temporary closings, or unforeseen business circumstances. Legal counsel on a company's ability to satisfy the law's requirements—which are more complicated than one might think from the brief description here—is important. That's because jurisdiction is in federal court, and penalties for noncompliance include back pay, benefits, and per diem fines.

Planning for the announcement should be outlined step-by-step in one document. Many law firms and PR firms have experience in this area. Detailed manuals and workbooks are available from trade organizations. Some law firms and HR consultants offer seminars that deal with the subject. But it is important that the public relations aspects of the announcements not be slighted while planning to meet the legal requirements.

The first priority is to maintain confidentiality until announcement day. Work with PR counsel to prepare a standby plan and press statement in case of leaks or rumors.

Develop a timetable of who will do what, when and where on announcement day. When and how will employees be informed? Who will notify state and local officials? Who will respond to media inquiries? Should key customers and suppliers be informed first by phone, in-person, letter, and/or email?

Develop a checklist of materials and activities for the day. These include employee information packets, paycheck stuffers, press releases, materials needed by outplacements consultants in meeting with employees, and so forth.

Spokespersons to media, customers, suppliers, local officials, and financial analysts, as well as executives making announcements to employees, should have scripts. They also should have lists of anticipated questions, with factual answers and suggested responses. These Q&A documents ensure all spokespeople are communicating the same basic facts. This practice also helps prepare them psychologically and emotionally for a difficult day.

Depending on the experience of the executives involved in the announcement, training and rehearsal of spokespersons will also be a useful step.

Announcement of the news should stress the positives as much as possible. If the company is offering generous severance benefits and outplacement counseling, this should be noted in the press release or statements. Companies that go the extra mile in seeking state placement assistance and private industry job opportunities, while providing terminated employees with assistance in interviewing and job-seeking skills, will gain much goodwill.

PHASE THREE: FOLLOW-UP

After an announcement such as this, there is a tendency to breathe a sigh of relief and get on with other things. But that is precisely the time when the need for follow-up is greatest.

The company should assess audience reactions to determine any lingering problems. What is employee reaction elsewhere in the company? How does the financial community view the closing? Where is the stock price heading? How did the business press handle the news? Was coverage in the trade press, social media and the local community media negative or even-handed?

The answers to these questions may reveal a need for further communications with key constituencies such as the financial community or trade press. For example, a follow-up meeting or call with financial analysts, bankers, and portfolio managers would be appropriate. Or management may need to update the trade press on the company's commitment to uninterrupted customer service and new corporate goals or strategies.

As with so many business challenges, the issues can be solved with candid disclosure, detailed planning and straightforward communications.

Keep in mind we have a changing culture with many different kinds of people from different ethnic and economic backgrounds you must interact with in many of these environments. When I was managing the plant closing discussed in the paragraphs above—a very large operation in central Indiana—the local sheriff gave the corporate executive making the announcement some advice that took us both by surprise. He thought the exec, standing up in front of hundreds of employees about to be told they were losing their livelihoods, should wear a bulletproof vest. Everybody in the room looked at me, as if to say, "Well, what do YOU think, Mr. PR exec?" And I'm thinking: I'm going to tell the county sheriff he's wrong? Suppose he's not? The corporate suit wore the bulletproof vest. What surprised us all was how many employees could tell he was wearing a bulletproof vest, which the sheriff had thoughtfully provided, from a distance.

I was once retained by a major retail chain to deal with local labor and community issues in the Bahamas. Layoffs and store closings would be taking place in some neighborhoods, but hiring and new store openings would take place elsewhere. There had been some minor vandalism of company property, such as smashed windows of delivery trucks, graffiti spray-painted on building walls, and similar incidents. It struck me first off that this would be a long-term program that really needed local expertise, much as I would have loved a long-term stay in the Bahamas at corporate expense. My initial recommendation was to hire a local fixer who knew local politicians, communities, and media. I found several promising candidates through an international public relations association group. During a week of planning and meetings, we interviewed several candidates and finally settled on a local professional who proved well up to the job. I concluded the week by helping with briefings and later offered advice and monitoring from stateside, but at that point the hand-off was largely completed. End result, a happy client.

By the way, I almost always take the advice of local law

enforcement. A question came up after the fatal shooting of several employees as part of a robbery in Georgia. The company wanted to offer a reward for people to come forward with information, what should the size of the reward be? That was an easy lateral: Ask the local police. They gave us a number, and that was the number we used. The number might have been quite different in another state or town.

In states such as Pennsylvania and Michigan, for example, deer-hunting with crossbows is quite popular. Disgruntled employees were shooting out the radiators of delivery trucks entering and leaving company production plants with crossbow bolts. Clearly at some point, somebody was likely to get hurt. State police were in sympathy with the malcontents and were doing nothing to resolve the situation. Some company video-taping of incidents through fixed cameras at the plants and hand-held cameras wielded by plant managers helped provide evidence—not for a court of law, but for insurance companies, state officials, media, and the National Labor Relations Board. A series of meetings initiated by local plant managers and citizens with the governor's office and authorities, with video at the ready, eventually would defuse tensions and restore equanimity.

In a different financial scenario, the CEO and founder of one of my micro-cap clients owned a large percentage of stock on which he collected millions in dividends each quarter. The stock was the frequent subject of positive and as well as vitriolic commentary on the condition of the company's business and the generous pay enjoyed by its executives. One string of posts on a social media investment website turned dark with actual death threats against the CEO and CFO. We notified the FBI.

Note these kinds of cases aren't the typical "slip and fall" cases that every casino, restaurant, or shop owner has to deal with. Most of these really are just elderly people, or drunks, or people take sick, who slip and fall, not fraud, and if the case ever becomes ugly, a financial settlement (sometimes just discounts or a free night at the casino hotel), make it go away.

In truth, a surprising number of incidents or potential incidents never make it out to the public in a big way. There was the restaurant chain where a manager of a local eatery went hiking with his wife and two employees, one of whom was apparently his girlfriend, and the wife disappeared. She was never found. There was no evidence of foul play. The story never made the news.

The woman who was rescued from the trunk of a car in a hotel lot was a big one-day local story in that town. I was the company spokesman for the incident. While it was short-lived, the effort taken to gather facts, work with local police, assemble and approve a statement through the corporate chain of authority, and answer questions from local media, was considerable.

Management is caught in the crossfire in every crisis situation. We've all seen the Miranda warning on countless cop shows, right? "Everything you say can and will be used against you."

That's good advice working with media, investors and any public venue.

Be careful what you say and do when cameras and recording devices may be around. Even if you don't see them, assume they are there.

Yes, good communications with customers, employees, financial analysts, media, community groups, and others is essential for your future success. Yet the company must be protected from the unwarranted intrusions or accidental disclosure of information in areas such as product development, new product introductions, acquisition or divestiture possibilities, and marketing plans.

No program for managing information is fail-safe, given immense amounts of data, photos and records available and the endless ways to obtain, copy, and distribute same. But options are available. Let's discuss several strategies.

Establish a companywide communications policy. Publicly held companies should already have a financial disclosure policy that determines which executives, under what circumstances, can provide sensitive information to the outside world. The purpose of this is to avoid selective disclosure which may trigger shareholder lawsuits or liability under the federal securities laws. A communications policy is much more inclusive.

What is necessary is to broaden our thinking about information management and the concept of disclosure to include corporate communications in general. Being transparent does not require us to be foolish. Understand that all information about the company—legally required materials and statements such as the Form 10-K, sales literature, annual reports, speeches by executives at trade association meetings, press releases including early drafts, internal memoranda, government filings, public relations and advertising plans—may become freely available to competitors seeking market intelligence, or to news media that will interpret it and influence public opinion. Managers need to understand the far-reaching effects of this full disclosure. They need to think about how to control and integrate the communications.

Make sure the organization's communications further its strategic mission. The potential availability of information is no reason to stop communicating. Organizations need to talk to the financial community. They need to market. They need to communicate with employees about company progress. But communications should be strategic—based on a mission and well-thought-out policies. Policies are decisions. College recruiting, sales plans, and credit policies are crafted with specific business objectives in mind, for example. Shouldn't corporate communications, including crisis plans, advertising, marketing, sales, and digital media efforts function on the same strategic level? The ideal is to integrate them so they share a common focus.

Consider company policies, actions and communications from the standpoint of other audiences. In other words, cover the bases. When executives make statements to the press, remember that the comments will be printed together with those of the financial and industry analysts. Communications-savvy managers understand that theirs is only one voice and, given the opportunity, refer media to the analysts or experts who best understand their company and industry.

Candid, timely disclosure wins points from consumers, the public, and government officials. It's come to be expected. Companies that fall short of the standard will be judged harshly.

Future trends indicate we will require more and more disclosure of corporate information, voluntarily or involuntarily, in normal times and in times of crisis. More demand for news. More information available to more and more people. Less time for corporate management to plan a response. In this environment, policies affecting content and disclosure of information represent major decisions affecting your corporate reputation. We don't have the luxury of retreating to Walden Pond like a Thoreau, but we do have the ability to manage with foresight and sensitivity, even in a full-disclosure society. This is how to master disaster.

As a CNN producer once told me, "Local media cover the house fires. We cover the block fire."

ValuJet and Boeing were block fires.

10
LESSONS FOR LEADERS

Now is the time of the disruptor. Big Tech, of course, disrupting industries and business models, pioneered by Silicon Valley. CEOs of all stripes are introducing new products and services, some truly revolutionary. Geopolitically, larger-than-life figures such as Donald Trump, Boris Johnson, Vladimir Putin, and Angela Merkel have made major policy changes that affected us all, in many cases clearly not for the better. Consultants with many different kinds of expertise appear regularly as bloggers and talking heads on cable TV. Many of these leaders and experts have a confidence, sometimes a swagger. Is this what you need to succeed in the business world? Is all publicity good publicity? Do you have to be a bully to succeed?

Clearly not. Many of today's well-known billionaires and disruptors exist outside the roles of the past. I often think of the mysterious creator of the bitcoin, Satoshi Nakamoto, who authored the original white paper on the subject—surely as famous as Milton Friedman's white paper arguing that the social responsibility of business is to increase its profits—and developed the first blockchain to support the roll-out. A bust with anonymous features was installed in his honor at a business park in Hungary in 2021, notable for the fact that his true identity is still unknown. In the corporate world, I've noticed a trend for senior executives to cultivate a calmer presence and to be much more affable, as if a switch to the spirit of the times has been clicked; perhaps leaders are reacting to the strong man model and pushing back. In arts and entertainment it is of course the duty of famous people to do things that make them famous, yet actor George Clooney's spouse Amal, an accomplished human rights attorney before her marriage, is better known than her actor husband. However all these trends work out in terms of individual style, it shows to me that many people have learned the key point of Jen Sincero's best-selling book, *You Are a Badass: How to Stop Doubting Your Greatness and Start Living an Awesome Life.*

Sincero argues that an awesome personal and professional life is built on confidence, performance and healthy goals, but to change your behavior you must go beyond wanting to do so and actually *decide* to do so. In different words, she is saying you must get intentional, as I've written earlier. And when she uses the word badass, I think she means to be a strong man or woman—but in a good way. In the world of ethics and compliance we would probably use the phrase "trusted adviser," "senior counselor," or "problem solver." "Disruptor" or "achiever" might be the words in popular nomenclature.

Inspired by Sincero's book and what I have learned as a consultant and lawyer, here are some additional thoughts that will help you become the world-class operator I know you can be. And then, as Sincero says, you can make some real money!

KEEP A TIGHT FOCUS ON YOUR GOALS

This may seem self-evident, but we can all point to countless examples of compliance plans that were neglected after the first month, or practitioners who lost track of their career goals. Somewhere, make a notation to revisit your goals on a periodic basis that works for you. The qualities that lead to success require more than attitude; goal-oriented performance is required.

For example, Didgebridge's John McNulty opined, "It's important to have a mission that's focused on solving major problems, and you have to be able to articulate that very quickly. And you need to be able to address very specific market segments. We have the overall consumer marketing sector, but the largest sector is marketing and communications within healthcare. We have proprietary technology specializing in mobile video communication. Our content does not travel through the public internet system, which in healthcare is very important. People in healthcare don't want to be searched, tracked, or have their data mined. This was a sweet spot because what we do is ultra-private consumer education, and in healthcare that's a big deal."

After all, to aspire is simply to seek to attain a goal. But that somewhat dry definition misses the point. To aspire implies a more noble or important mission than an average goal. It suggests a desire or motivation so important as to even be noble, at least as far as the individual holding it is concerned. Apple founder Steve Jobs had the goal of delivering easy computing power to the masses. Steve Jobs' goal of democratizing computing motivated him personally and professionally, ultimately involving thousands, even millions, in his personal vision, and creating one of the world's most valuable brands.

But those who enjoy its beautifully designed smartphones, laptops and other products embrace its product mystique and usability that have powered the company's atmospheric stock price.

Most of us will not revolutionize an industry. All of us, however, have some aspiration. Some want to be world-class skaters. Some want the recognition and paycheck of the next promotion. An executive burnt out on corporate chaos longs for the freedom of running his or her own shop. For a homeless person, it may only be to attain a $30 hotel room to spend the night in safely. We can't let others define our goals for us or let ourselves be swayed to look at our own goals as too modest or even demeaning.

Aspirations may be large or small, personal or professional or corporate, short-term or long-term, very specific or very general. Aspirations can be quite unique to yourself—exceeding your "personal best" in a half-marathon or publishing your first novel. They can be quite specific—managing the family budget to give a 10% tithe to church, or a $1,000 donation to a no-kill pet shelter. They can be quite general, such as "become a better husband and father" or "find a better job with like-minded people who share my values, while providing for my financial security." Or, they may be both personal and societal. The female CEO of tech consultant Accenture opined on a national business TV program that before more women would become members of senior management, "more women must aspire to become CEOs."

Some examples? Investment banker Vernon E. Jordan is called "Mr. Strategy" for a reason. Hollywood agent Ed Limato was called "the velvet hammer" for his ability to make clients happy while meeting their business goals. I once watched a legendary consultant charm a tough manager at a Fortune 100 company simply by handing him a business card, making a note, and saying, "That's my private number. Call me anytime." You can bet this notoriously hard-to-please executive did so and got good advice.

An executive at a well-known consumer tech company had to go completely back to basics when the company abandoned the growth strategy announced at the investor roadshows when it went public. He had to rebuild credibility internally and externally but set about educating management about the contributions of compliance with new goals and timelines. Slowly, he is succeeding.

DON'T BE THE LONE RANGER

Across all the senior executives interviewed for this book, the real importance of teamwork and trusted advisors is one overarching theme. It's true regardless of company size but is especially critical for the young company.

Didgebridge CEO John McNulty observed, "I've done some consulting work with early-stage startup-up companies and tried to apply those principles to my work at Didgebridge. You may be inclined to think you can do everything yourself, but you can't. Most entrepreneurs think they can be the first baseman, the third baseman, and the shortstop all at once. You can't; you need a team, so I brought in a team with individual expertise. You need experts in finance, operations, sales, marketing, etc."

How can a fledgling operation afford so many people?

McNulty again: "You can't put them all at the table at once because you won't have the money, but you can grant equity in the company, allow them to purchase equity, and incentivize them for sales on a commission basis so they have the opportunity to get cash. You can't expect people to work for free."

In other words, yell for help.

CONTROL YOUR EMOTIONS

We are often tasked with delivering bad news to senior management. A top executive at a major consumer company once picked up his phone and threw it at a good friend of mine who had come to him with some bad corporate news. A trade journal called my friend to ask about the story, and concerned about the reputation of both the company and the executive, he denied it. Of course, the phone-throwing senior executive would have been hugely embarrassed (and in trouble with HR) if the incident had surfaced. Was it the right call? By most lights, no. But my friend has never regretted it.

That said, ruling and using your emotions can be a powerful advantage. A close colleague once faked a temper tantrum during a marathon-length merger meeting and threatened to end the negotiations. The other party immediately ceded ground. The talks were back on.

FIND A MENTOR OR COACH

Early in my career, at the international consulting firm Burson-Marsteller, I had the privilege of working with co-founder Harold Burson on several major accounts. One thing I noticed immediately at client luncheons is that Harold always had his notebook out taking notes while the CEO or CFO was speaking, while my peers continued to eat lunch and listen. Guess who I chose as a role model.

Find a mentor or coach, somebody to learn and emulate, regardless of your age or professional station. Ideally, it's somebody in your profession or one closely related, that you can meet in person and observe, preferably in a formalized relationship. But this is not essential. It might be anyone you admire for various professional achievements or qualities of character. In addition to Harold Burson—one of the politest people I've ever met—I have other role models in all walks of life who inspire me by the trials they have endured and the contributions they make to improve this world.

PREPARE FOR ANYTHING

After ValuJet was rebranded as AirTran following the crash of flight 592 in the Everglades, settlement negotiations with the families of those lost continued for five years while new management changed stock exchanges, held annual meetings, and opened new markets. Management developed a contingency plan in case litigants held demonstrations at company events. Of course, great sensitivity would be important given the loss these family members had suffered. As it turned out, the contingency plans were never implemented, but the planning provided peace of mind and could have avoided a potential public relations disaster.

In 2019, as senators grilled Boeing's CEO over the 737 Max jet crashes, still photos and TV footage showed people who held photos of loved ones who died in crashes sitting behind him. Such images can prove long-lasting and deeply troubling, especially if taken out of context. I once nixed a photo op requested by a prominent publication of Humana's CEO standing outside the glitzy corporate headquarters of Humana, with the company name emblazoned prominently on the walls of the building. I suspected the story that was being prepared would be largely negative, and the last thing we wanted would be the implication the company wasted money on bricks and mortar or that company management was oblivious to public healthcare but not to corporate ego. My concern proved well-founded, and that was one photo.

DON'T LOOK BACK IN ANGER

American business is very introspective, and in my experience personal and professional introspection is an essential part of finding your way in life. That said, many of us look back on the way we handled fast-moving pressure situations in a negative fashion. Beating yourself up by asking *why did I use that word*, or *I wish I had thought of something different to say*, just builds anxiety about your own professional ability. If you think you made a mistake, try to put it behind you quickly, learn a lesson from it, and move on quickly. The most successful senior executives make a point of doing this. It seems to help them immeasurably in their careers.

SOMETIMES, YOU JUST HAVE TO BOGART YOUR WAY THROUGH

An important trait in a badass, by the way, is a knack for using nouns as verbs. Therefore, when all else fails and you don't know what to do, just Bogart your way through. While Bogart isn't usually a word associated with legal or business matters, consider Bogie's ability to boldly and coolly steal any scene. His style and self-confidence always puts him in a good place. Trust in your proven ability to do what needs to be done. The motto of the professional society *Les Clefs d'Or* is to do "whatever is legal and kind." Those are words to live and work by.

ACKNOWLEDGMENTS

This book began in the hurly-burly of daily consulting with business founders, owners, managers, and leaders of all stripes. Recognizing these individuals along with others inspirational figures may be a long list but since this may be my only book, now is the time. First and foremost, I want to thank my wife, Deborah, my partner in all things and a talented author in her own right, for being a beta reader and for being so supportive of this effort. Thanks also to my fantastic children, Caitlin and Doug, the world traveler and the philosopher, respectively, who help make every day worth living, as do the newest member of our family, Lexi, and the furriest, Indigo.

Many people helped make this a better book, including beta readers Lisa Ciota and Rene Caron, both supremely qualified corporate counselors; my editor, Martha Reineke, cover illustrators Peter and Caroline O'Connor and our formatting professional, Andrew Chapman. Also weighing in were content contributors such as close friend, client and serial startup creator Mike Marcus; dealmaker extraordinaire Jeff Temple of Peakstone; Charlie Funk of MidWestOne Financial Group, the CEO every CEO should aspire to be; Steve Eschbach, of Transworld Business Advisors; Stuart Dixon of VentureDNA, the boutique advisor I like to call "Mr. Strategy;" and digital entrepreneur John McNulty of Didgebridge.

While I'm at it, I'd also like to thank several people for their friendship and moral support: Sean Murphy of Inside 8; the late Grayson Mitchell and Al Smedley; Harlan Teller, a dedicated mentor to myself and many others; Joanne Tremulis, my first good boss; Steve Lundin, corporate fixer and brand advisor to the private equity world; the late Joe Allen, multidisciplinary corporate financial expert and mystery writer (perhaps the two worlds are closer than we think); Mike Mason, who successful navigated the transition from investor relations to investment banking; Bianca Fersini Mastelloni, president and CEO of Rome-based POLYTEMS HIR Srl; Chip Avery and Philip Kranz of Power-Solutions International; and anyone I did not mention here but should have!

NOTES

Introduction

Anheuser-Busch stock tanked, Bud light sales, Brooke DiPalma, "Bud Light sales keep slipping in another very weak week," *Yahoo!Finance*, 6 June 6 2023. See also: Chip Cutter and Lauren Weber, "Companies Rethink Embrace of Social Issues," *The Wall Street Journal*, p. 1, 7 June 2023.

eliminated the grid girls, Cyril Matlock, "Taking the Sex out of Sports in Europe," *Bloomberg Business Week*, 19 February 2018.

1: MANAGING IN A FULL DISCLOSURE WORLD

the value of investor relations, Belotti, Asgarval, Nash and Toffler, "Does IR Add Value?" 23 October 2010. See also Brad Samson, "The Link between Good Investor Relations and Stock Price," *CFO Magazine*, 17 June 2017.

the misrepresentations involved, David Halberstam, *The Best and The Brightest*, The Modern Library, New York, 1969, p. 648

IPO definition, Jason Zweig, *The Devil's Financial Dictionary*, 30 September 2015

"I had an exit plan..." Steve Eschbach, interview with the author, November 2019

2: DE-MYSTIFYING SHAREHOLDER VALUE

Investor relations definition, "Standards of Practice for Investor Relations" National Investor Relations Institute, 6 February 2023, p. 2.

3: REPUTATION MANAGEMENT IN A DIGITAL AGE

Warren Buffett observations on reputation, Marcel Schwantes, *Inc.*, 6 November 2021

"the problem they had is a massive..." Patrick Coffee, "Crypto Brands Remake Images Following FTX, Market Tumble," *Wall Street Journal*, 7 February 2023, p. B2

"the name didgebridge," John McNulty, interview with the author, January 2020

4: BRANDING FOR SUCCESS

three networks then, Margaret Sullivan, "Journalists Can't Repeat Their Watergate Hero Role," *Washington Post*, 9 June 2019

Boeing at Paris Air Show, "Boeing CEO Swaps Air Show Swagger for Humility," Bloomberg, 16 June 2019

information expands, Harlan Cleveland, "Information as a Resource," *Futurist,* December 2019, pp. 34-39

corporate social responsibility, Brian O'Connell, "A New Era in Corporate Responsibility," *Society for Human Resource Management Journal,* 4 January 2020

Mark Rosenbloom and InspireTV, *Pioneer Press, Chicago Tribune,* December 11, 2017

5: FAMILY TIES

"couldn't afford to hire one," Jim Boccarosso, in part citing his wife Stephanie, interview with the author at a restaurant, December 2019

"closely held businesses often fail to understand the range of options," Jeff Temple, interview with the author, November 2019

invasive due diligence, Jeff Temple, interview with the author, November 2019

"a disaster for manufacturing," "Program Aims to Help Chicago Manufacturers Find Successors," Associated Press, 18 January 2019

foundry and casting industry, American Foundry Society, annual meeting, Chicago, 13 February 2020

importance of advisors, Jeff Temple, interview with the author, December 2019

bringing in a trusted advisor, Steve Eschbach, interview with the author, January 2020

"the company was founded," Charlie Funk, series of interviews, 2019

Growth of MidWestOne Financial Group, Charlie Funk, phone and email interviews with the author, 2019

"only one member of the family serves on the board," interview with Charlie Funk, November 2019

importance of scale, growth through acquisition, Charlie Funk, interview with the author, November 2019

current plans, Charlie Funk, phone and email interviews with the author, 2017-2020

"there does have to be a solution," Steve Eschbach, interview with the author, February 2020

6: UNICORNS, BULLS AND BEARS

making calculations in the temple, Sun Tzu, *The Art of War*, Penguin Books, 1992, p.6

unicorn valuations, Sharon Goldman, *VentureBeat,* 27 June 2022, available at https://venturebeat.com

IPO plans of startups, Angus Loten, "Uncertain Markets have Startups Rethinking IPOs," quoting Techstars, *The Wall Street Journal*, May 1, 2023, p.1.

IPO tracker, *Stock Analysis*, June 7, 2023, available at https://stockanalysis.com.

seed investments dropped, *Pitchbook-NCVA Venture Monitor*, October 2022, p. 8

"as we have evolved," John McNulty, interview with the author, January 2019

"internal knowledge of capital markets," Adam J. Epstein, statistic cited with the author in an email, 11 June 2023

"decision is based on people," Stewart Dixon, interview with the author, January 2020

"we are a coach with a whistle," Stewart Dixon, interview with the author, January 2020

7: THE ABCs of IPOs

board approved 1-for-20 stock split, Bruce Japsen, "Rite Aid Board Approves Reverse Stock Split to Avoid NYSE Delisting," *Forbes*, 10 April 2019

8: CASHING IN ON CANNABIS

"pot of gold," Tara Lachapelle and Rani Mola, "Pot of Gold," *Bloomberg Business Week*, 15 October 2018

"the numbers are amazing," Centers for Disease Control, available at https://www.cdc.gov/data/statistics

legal and illegal market, Grandview Research, available at Grandviewresearch.com/industry-analysis/legal-marijuana-market

Altria becomes largest shareholder in Cronos, Securities & Exchange Commission, available at https://www.sec.gov.Archives/edgardata, 8 March 2019

Pax Labs completes financings, Crunchbase, https://www.crunchbase.com/company-financings

Illegal market in California, "The Black Market Strangled California's Legal Weed Industry," available at https://www.politico.com/news

"weed is legal in New York but the illegal market is still booming," PBS, available at *https:www.pbs.orgnewshour/nation/weed-is-legal-in-new York-but-the-illegal-market-is-still booming-here's why*

Harvest Health acquires Verano Holdings, "Chicago-based Cannabis Operator Verano Acquired by Harvest Health," *Daily Herald*, available at https://www.dailyherald.com/business

CBD Lion acquired, "Acquired Sales Corp. Signs Definitive Merger Agreement to Acquire 100% of CBD Lion LLC," press release, 20 August 2019.

9: BE A MASTER OF DISASTER

Research presented to ValuJet board of directors by Cramer-Krasselt agency,

Tom Duncan, "AirTran: How IMC Helped Build a Brand," and *IMC: Using Advertising Promotion to Build Brands,* McGraw-Hill Irvin, 2002, p. 4

"Overnight, share price rebounded," Tom Duncan, "AirTran: How IMC Helped Build a Brand," *IMC: Using Advertising and Promotion to Build Brands,* McGraw-Hill Irwin, 2002, p. 7

10: LESSONS FOR LEADERS

"make some real money," Jen Sincero, *You Are A Badass!,* Running Press Book Publishers, 17 October 2017, p. 201

"important to have a mission," John McNulty, interview with the author, January 2020

"important to have more females in management," Julie Sweet, Accenture CEO, in interview with CNN Business, 23 April 23 2018.

"you need a team," John McNulty, interview with the author, January 2020

ABOUT THE AUTHOR

Steve Carr is a pioneer in corporate strategic counseling and a specialist in tough assignments. His advice has appeared in major media and helped management teams grow their businesses around the world. He speaks about reputation management issues regularly to investors, companies, trade groups and other interested audiences.